# History of the Liturgy

## The Major Stages

*Marcel Metzger*

French text
translated by

*Madeleine Beaumont*

*A Liturgical Press Book*

THE LITURGICAL PRESS
Collegeville, Minnesota

Cover design by David Manahan, O.S.B.

This book was originally published in French by Desclée de Brouwer, Paris, France, under the title *Histoire de la liturgie: Les grandes étapes* © 1994 by Desclée de Brouwer.

Library of Congress Cataloging-in-Publication Data

Metzger, Marcel.
    [Histoire de la liturgie. English]
    History of the liturgy : the major stages / Marcel Metzger ;
French text translated by Madeleine M. Beaumont.
        p.   cm.
    Includes bibliographical references and index.
    ISBN 0-8146-2433-2
    1. Catholic Church—Liturgy—History and criticism. 2. Liturgics.
I. Title.
BX1970.M48413    1997
264'.02—dc21
                                                              96-51700
                                                                    CIP

# Contents

# Introduction

"When you have brought the people out of Egypt, you shall worship God on this mountain" (Exod 3:12). This word is one of the revelations Moses received on Mount Horeb, or Sinai, in the episode of the burning bush (Exod 3). This word was read anew after the Christian Pasch, in Stephen's discourse, but with an allusion to the Temple: ". . . and after that they shall come out and worship me in this place" (Acts 7:7).

The whole mystery of the Covenant is revealed in these few words. God had manifested the divine self to Abraham and his descendants, then to Moses and the people God had freed from the slavery of Egypt and the golden calf: God had made the divine self known and had established a unique and jealous relationship with this people. The dictates recorded in the Book of Deuteronomy unceasingly refer to this relationship: "So now, O Israel, what does the LORD your God require of you? Only to fear the LORD your God, to walk in all his ways, to love him, to serve the LORD your God with all your heart and with all your soul, and to keep the commandments of the LORD your God and his decrees that I am commanding you today, for your own well-being (Deut 10:12-13; see also 6:13; 10:20; 11:13; 13:4; Jos 22:5; 14-24; and so forth).

The people responded to the proposed Covenant by "serving" God. At first, in the same way as other peoples, by rendering God a sacrificial worship. In Moses' bargaining with Pharaoh, under the pressure of the ten plagues, this sort of worship was presented as the principal reason for leaving Egypt: "Let us go a three days' journey into the wilderness to sacrifice to the LORD our God, or he will fall upon us with pestilence or sword" (Exod 5:3; see also 3:18; 7:16; 8:1; 8:8, 20, 27; 9:1, 13; 10:3, 24). In this narrative, God's service is thus explained: "Let my people serve me, let it sacrifice to the LORD."

1

The Book of Leviticus describes in detail the numerous sacrifices by which the priestly class served God in the name of
the people. These rituals were still practiced in Jesus' time, and
Zechariah, the father of John the Baptist, took part in them in
his turn (Luke 1:8-10). Every day, animals were offered in the
Temple precincts on the altar of sacrifices. One served God by
giving God food, by reserving the choice parts of the victim
which were burned and went up in smoke, supposed to reach
God's nostrils as a pleasing odor (Gen 8:21; Exod 29:18; Lev
1:9; and so forth).

But Jesus' coming completely overturned the status quo:
beginning with the Last Supper, on the eve of the Passion-
Resurrection of God's Son, it is God who gives food to God's
people and opens God's table to them. Of course, this innovation had been announced by prophets and sages for a long
time (Isa 55; Prov 9:5; and so forth). However, since the
Resurrection (Mark 16:14; John 21:12-13; and so forth), the
New Covenant is made present in Jesus, the true bread come
down from heaven (John 6:51), under the form of a meal, from
Sunday to Sunday, until the day of the eternal nuptials (Matt
25:1-13). Jesus is the Servant of the Father, and he leads his
people into the new service of God; but at the same time, an
unheard-of thing, he, the Master, serves at table (Luke 12:37).
With him, the "service" of God is radically transformed.

> In summary, we see that "to serve God" is not only to perform
> acts of worship; it is to commit the whole person in all the acts
> of one's life. Although worship is the highest form of the "serv-
> ice of God," the latter runs the gamut from manual work to
> adoration in prayer. . . .
>
> Thus, the "service" has become a constellation of qualities
> of heart and mind, of the whole person; an attitude and a prac-
> tice animated by a deep faith; a religious sentiment that per-
> meates one's entire life, expressed by self-giving, devotion to
> others, attentive obedience, perfect faithfulness. This "service"
> is the very activity of love, the generous search for the beloved
> Lord, the eagerness to "observe God's commands." These are
> words and realities of the Old Testament which will find their
> fulfillment in the New. Jesus will be the "Servant of God" par
> excellence. And "in Christ Jesus," his disciples, the Christians,
> can also, if they so wish, "serve" God in truth.[1]

At the end of a patient evolution, directed by God's pedagogy, the manifestations of the Covenant are no longer limited to bloody sacrifices, offered solely by the priestly class. God's communication with God's new people, priestly in its entirety, is realized within the setting of a meal of communion with all its components: sharing of the word, the bread, and the wine. The liturgy of the New Covenant not only replaces the sacrificial worship of the Temple, but appropriates the morning and evening offices of readings, blessings, and prayers of the Synagogue. The long conversation of Jesus with his disciples at the Last Supper (John 13–17) shows to what degree the New Covenant is God's revelation to God's people, communion with God's Spirit through words and dialogue within the framework of the breaking of the bread.

Although the new sacrifice was accomplished once for all (Heb 7:26-27) by the eternal high priest, Jesus Christ, it is rendered present in the Church's time. Thus, the New Covenant is the heart of the Christian mystery. Its realization in the present is effected in the Church's Eucharist—which is the preeminent Sunday liturgy—and also in the totality of ecclesial celebrations—in the first place the daily liturgy of the hours.

Therefore, the term "liturgy" designates this vast and deep movement which begins with Abel's sacrifice and culminates with Christ's and by which God renders present the Covenant with God's people. In human history, liturgy appears from the beginning because the whole of God's enterprise—what is called the economy of salvation—has for its goal communication between God and God's people, the very reason God created humankind: God took the first steps. Afterwards, all through the Old Testament, there took place a long preparation: God's people were led to progressively transform the cultic usages taken over from their environment so that these usages would be fit to welcome the New Covenant and become the instrument and place of its realization.

> In the Symbol of the faith the Church confesses the mystery of the Holy Trinity and of the plan of God's "good pleasure" (Eph 1:9) for all creation: the Father accomplishes the "mystery of his will" by giving his beloved Son and his Holy Spirit for the salvation of the world and for the glory of his name. Such is the

mystery of Christ, revealed and fulfilled in history according to the wisely ordered plan that St. Paul calls the "plan of the mystery" (Eph 3:9) and the patristic tradition will call the "economy of the Word incarnate" or the "economy of salvation.". . . For this reason, the Church celebrates in the liturgy above all the Paschal mystery by which Christ accomplished the work of our salvation.

It is the mystery of Christ that the Church proclaims and celebrates in her liturgy so that the faithful may live from it and bear witness to it in the world.[2]

There is nothing whatever, there is no benefit which is available to [human beings] by their reconciliation with God, which has not been bestowed through Him who has been appointed the Mediator between God and [humanity] [see 1 Tim 2:5]. [God] has given us no other means whatever by which we may find the Mediator and lay hold of Him and receive what is His than the Mysteries [the liturgy]. They make us His [kin] in His Blood, partakers of the graces which He received through His flesh, and partakers of the sufferings which He endured. . . . If we are thus with Christ by sacred rite, prayer, meditation, and reflection, we shall train the soul for every virtue. As Paul commands, we shall "guard what has been entrusted to us" [1 Tim 6:20; 2 Tim 1:12, 14] and preserve the grace which has been imparted to us from the Mysteries. It is Christ Himself who initiates us in His Mysteries; He Himself is the content of the Mysteries. Likewise it is He who preserves His gifts in us. It is He alone who enables us to abide in that which we have received, for as He says, "apart from me you can do nothing" [John 15:5].[3]

The liturgy is the actualization of the New Covenant, accomplished by the ecclesial community through Christ, mediator between God and humankind, in the Holy Spirit, under the appearances of efficacious signs and according to a legitimate order.[4]

The use of the word "liturgy" to designate this central aspect of the Christian mystery is rather recent, dating back barely two centuries. Before that, people spoke of sacred rites, ceremonies, offices, and so on. Besides, the Roman church finds itself in a peculiar situation because after the first millennium, liturgy underwent a slow drift, with, at intervals, attempts at adaptation to changed circumstances. Then, the liturgical renewal came about, gaining strength in the first half of the twentieth century, receiving the seal of approval at Vatican II, and thus allowing for a fundamental and general reform in the Roman church. This evolution does not go without meeting with some resistance and also suffering "relapses." Never will the liturgical reform be regarded as completed since it is one of the fundamental components of pastoral work, which is effected by the Spirit in the Church.

With Jesus, the long preparation for the New Covenant reached its completion. Was this in order to inaugurate an era of total immobility? By no means! Indeed, just as an example, how many differences exist between the Last Supper and our Eucharists of today: the setting, the action (meal or gathering), the number and placement of the participants—all this has changed. In fact, in the course of the centuries, the celebration of the New Covenant has been organized according to material resources, mental and cultural categories, and socio-political circumstances of Christian communities. One can observe that every period changes the equilibrium between these various components. Since the time of the Apostles, community leaders have taken initiatives, under the guidance of the Holy Spirit, in order to innovate, to create new institutions and to adapt the celebrations to the concrete circumstances of their communities.

As a consequence, the aim of this brief history of the liturgy is to present the main phases of the evolution undergone by the Christian liturgy. We shall begin with an introduction to the sources that allow us to reconstruct this history. Then, we shall study the development of the liturgical institutions and distinguish in it five main stages that correspond to the situations of the churches in ancient, medieval, and modern societies:

1. The apostolic period, roughly the first century of our era, until the death of the Apostles, whose mandate is unique since they are direct witnesses of Jesus according to Acts 1:21-22.

2. The period of minorities and semi-clandestinity until the beginning of the fourth century. The churches do not have any public status; the communities are fairly small; and Christian institutions, including the liturgy, have not yet undergone significant regional diversifications throughout the Empire.

3. The "Peace of the Church," which grants public status to the churches in the Empire, fosters their growth, and organizes the collaboration between Empire and Church. This evolution is accomplished in several steps, and also in different ways in the East and the West. Institutions necessary to large communities are developed.

4. The period of the conversion of peoples as a result of the conversion of their leaders. Institutions are modified to promote the Christianization of rapidly baptized masses.

5. The period of stability, rigidity, renewals, and reforms of the Roman liturgy, from the end of the Middle Ages to Vatican II.

# Chapter 1

# The Historical Study of the Liturgy

The historical study of the liturgy was officially recognized by Vatican II, which prescribed, on the one hand, that it be integrated into the formation for pastoral ministries and religious life and, on the other, that it be used as a guide for all liturgical reforms (*Constitution on the Liturgy,* nos. 16, 23). The liturgy is indeed at the heart of the tradition of the Church; it is an apostolic heritage transmitted in a living way from generation to generation down to us. Whereas in a democracy the laws must obtain the assent of the majority, in the churches they must correspond to the will of Christ, the founder, as expressed in the tradition of the Church, written and oral. Therefore, the history of tradition, whose heart is the liturgy, is the place where the will of Christ the founder was manifested and was implemented by church leaders under the action of the Holy Spirit. As a consequence, the history of the liturgy must be known to church leaders, but it also interests believers eager to know the foundations of their faith.

The historical study consists in examining the different states of liturgical institutions in order to discern how traditions have evolved, and to discover what is fundamental, because instituted by Christ and the apostles, and what has been adapted or added in the course of the centuries, as required by pastoral necessity.

Like biblical sciences, the historical study of the liturgy appeals to the intellect (which we recognize as a gift from God) and to faith. On the one hand, this study must be conducted according to the rules of historical sciences by the analysis of the available documents and of the milieux from which they came. At the same time, in the history of Christian institutions, believers are led to recognize the traces of the Holy Spirit, who guides the churches. In any case, the liturgical celebrations themselves always include a look at history: through the readings, the preaching, and the thanksgivings, they uncover the realizations of the mystery of salvation in human situations, past and present.

Following the rules of this type of study, the history of liturgical institutions begins by the examination of the documents that have come down to us. Speaking of which, when we add up all the calamities that have befallen the churches in the course of the first millennium, we are astonished that a few witnesses of the past are still at our disposal. It is only too easy to recall the occasions and causes of destruction: persecutions, looting following the barbarian invasions and Islamic expansion, the iconoclastic crisis (that is, the quarrel concerning images in the Byzantine East from 726 to 843), the evil deeds of crusaders in Constantinople, earthquakes, fires. One should not forget either the destruction that can be termed natural, through the wear and tear on the books destined not to remain in good order in libraries but to pass from hand to hand for repeated use. As a result, the vestiges that have escaped the various causes of destruction and the deterioration due to time represent only a part, sometimes extremely small, of the monuments and writings that may have existed in a given place at a given time.

Furthermore, modern Christians who want to study the liturgy of the first centuries must turn a real mental somersault. They are so used to written rituals, complete and obligatory, that they risk projecting the present mode of functioning onto the first centuries of the Church. The truth is that for the first millennium, the liturgy was organized according to practices other than our own: oral tradition and institutional autonomy were the rule. For this reason, the available documentation concerning the early centuries is perforce limited, and its interpretation is the more difficult as one is constantly wondering whether it amounts to a sufficiently representative sample.

## The Oral Tradition

Christian institutions were formed in milieus of oral culture at a time when books, rare as well as expensive, were available only to the educated elites. With the Scriptures as their basic text, Christian communities preserved, developed, and transmitted their essential traditions through memory. Similarly, the order of celebrations was decided upon by each local church; it was not the result of the appropriation of written codes brought in from elsewhere but of the faithfulness to interiorized traditions.

Thus, the liturgies of the first centuries proclaimed the instructions and prayers in a living manner, according to schemes that had become traditional and were transmitted from memory. For instance, in the ancient general intercessions, the guidance given by the deacons (announcement of intentions), and the concluding prayers, one can see both striking resemblances and differences: the prayer intentions and their order are nearly identical but their formulation is variable.

The setting down in writing of the instructions and liturgical prayers was accomplished at a later date for various reasons: initiatives taken on account of theological conflicts, need for models, memorization, and other causes of which we are still ignorant. The need for writing down liturgical texts had already been recognized for the New Testament.

> In the beginning, the written word was only an auxiliary of the living memory. From the moment when the preachers of the gospel were no longer the direct witnesses and hearers of the words that were reported and the events that had occurred, it was useful for them to have memory aids in order to ensure the overall faithfulness of their preaching. They were not the originators of the transmitted tradition, but only their reporters, with all the flexibility which the adaptation of their teaching to the local communities required. It is noteworthy that the recourse to oral tradition alongside the reading of written collections was maintained well into the second century.[1]

## Ancient Witnesses of the Tradition in the Liturgical Domain

The Apostle Paul referred to oral tradition, now concerning his preaching (1 Cor 15:3; 2 Thess 3:6), now concerning liturgical

usages (1 Cor 11:23). In the same way, for several centuries
more, preachers and bishops attested to the importance oral
tradition still had in their time, in particular in the liturgical
domain, as shown by Basil the Great (d. 379).

> Concerning the teachings of the Church, whether publicly pro-
> claimed (*kerygma*) or reserved to members of the household of
> faith *(dogmata)*, we have received some from written sources,
> while others have been given to us secretly, through apostolic
> tradition. . . . For instance (to take the first and most common
> example), where is the written teaching that we should sign
> with the sign of the Cross those who, trusting in the Name of
> Our Lord Jesus Christ, are to be enrolled as catechumens?
> Which book teaches us to pray facing the East? Have any saints
> left for us in writing the words to be used in the invocation over
> the Eucharistic bread and the cup of blessing? As everyone
> knows, we are not content in the liturgy simply to recite the
> words recorded by St. Paul and the Gospels, but we add other
> words both before and after, words of great importance for this
> mystery. We have received these words from unwritten teach-
> ing. We bless the baptismal water and the oil for chrismation as
> well as the candidate approaching the font. By what written au-
> thority do we do this, if not from secret and mystical tradition?
> . . . . Are not all these things found in unpublished and un-
> written teachings, which our fathers guarded in silence, safe
> from meddling and petty curiosity? They had learned their les-
> son well; reverence for the mysteries is best encouraged by si-
> lence (*On the Holy Spirit* 27.65-66).[2]

The oral tradition was a factor of stability, as attested by St.
Cyprian of Carthage.

> I am fully aware, dearly beloved brother, that for the most part
> bishops who by the grace of God have been set in charge over
> the Lord's churches throughout the world adhere faithfully to
> the gospel truth and the Lord's teachings; they do not, by
> adopting any newfangled and [human] inventions, deviate
> from what Christ our Master prescribed and practiced. . . .
> And so . . . neither the Apostle himself nor an angel from
> heaven is at liberty to proclaim any doctrine different from that
> which Christ once taught and His apostles have proclaimed
> (*Letter 63* 1.1; 11.1).[3]

During the first three centuries, Christian institutions, including the liturgy, develop in parallel fashion in different churches. Established around the Mediterranean basin and within the Roman Empire, these communities are connected by the fact they belong to one and the same culture and by the relative facility of communications, especially by sea routes, of which the imperial administration was the guarantor. Because Christianity was born in Palestine and developed primarily among Eastern "immigrants" of the great cities of the Empire, the first centers where traditions originated were chiefly Eastern and their influence extended to more distant Western cities. Famous Christians, known by their literary works, followed a similar itinerary. Justin was born in Palestine, was converted to the Christian faith about 132, probably in Ephesus, and afterwards came to Rome. Irenaeus had been associated with Polycarp in Smyrna before sojourning in Rome and settling in Lyons, where he became the leader of the Christian community about 177.

Greek was the common language of the first churches, including that of Rome, until the third century. We possess a vestige of this, the *Kyrie eleison,* a prayer that had grown so familiar that it remained in use even after the Latin language had become again the usual tongue in Rome.

## The Archeological Vestiges

Archeological researches have provided some witnesses to the liturgy by studying the plan, arrangement, and decoration of ancient buildings or the remains of monuments, paintings, mosaics, and sculptures. Some of the main sites are Dura-Europos (east of present-day Syria), Ravenna, Rome, Syria, North Africa. The dimensions and arrangement of places of worship furnish information on the size of the assemblies, and the placement of the altar, seats, pulpits, doors, and so forth show how these assemblies were organized. Miniatures, illuminations and bindings of manuscripts, gold work and fabrics also have yielded clues by illustrating some moments of the liturgical celebrations.

## The Written Sources

The writings which allow us to know the history of the liturgy are diverse. The first one is the Bible, and this for two reasons: it is the source of the liturgical readings and it gives us the first testimonies on Christian celebrations. Among the other written documents, we will distinguish those which regulate the liturgy and those which describe it or mention it in passing. (The references will be supplied in the following chapters where these documents are quoted).

**The Church Orders.** The most ancient church orders deal with various questions concerning the organization of Christian communities and, as a consequence, include sections relative to the liturgy. As the oral tradition was preponderant, the purpose of these documents was limited to particular questions. This is evident in the *Didache,* the most ancient text of Christian teaching known to us, and close to the apostolic times: in the section on the organization of communities, only the points offering difficulties are discussed (see pp. 25–27). However, we have no knowledge of the sort of reception these rulings met with, that is, in what measure the communities applied them.

**The Commentaries on Rituals.** In catechesis and homilies, the preachers at times described systematically the rituals or certain aspects of the celebrations, at times merely alluded to them; this depended upon what was needed for the instruction of the catechumens and neophytes, or for ordinary preaching. In any case, what we have are direct testimonies on actual practices. We will return to this point later on, pp. 67 and ff.

We gathered other evocations or allusions from theological or pastoral treatises, such as those of Tertullian, Ambrose, John Chrysostom, Augustine, and others; from letters, in particular, Cyprian's; and from travel accounts, like that of Egeria, who in about 381 described the Jerusalem liturgy.

## The Method Followed for This Historical Study

In the following chapters, we will present the liturgical institutions as the available sources allow us to know them, according to the periods and the churches. To achieve this, we will examine the extant documents in order to reconstruct, as far as possible, the unfolding and evolution of rituals and formularies.

We will be careful to shed all apriorities and prejudices, distancing ourselves from certain methods which were all too common in the still recent past when the history of the liturgy was at the service of the demonstration of theses, and therefore, was utilized in a deductive way. Numerous examples of these deviations can be found in old treatises of sacramental theology. The writers of such books started from definitions worked out by medieval theology or the Council of Trent and applied these categories to liturgical institutions of previous periods.

The most famous example is that of the assumed antiquity of private confession. The controversy developed at the time of the Protestant Reformation as a sequel to the opposition to auricular confession. Some Catholic theologians affirmed at the Council of Trent and afterwards that private confession was in use in the Church from the beginning, and they believed they could prove it with the aid of the texts. They proceeded to stretch the available testimonies and to give them a faulty interpretation. As a result, historical research went astray for some time.

Since the ancient testimonies spoke only of the forgiveness of grave sins by public penance (see p. 57 and pp. 104–105), a debate arose concerning the pardon of other sins. Moreover, some theologians strove to prove that this pardon was reserved to priests who would have granted it in a "private" manner. The following quote contains an echo of these demonstrations which take their point of departure from dogmatic definitions, among which are those of the Council of Trent, on the obligation to have recourse to sacraments.

> If there were no private penance before the seventh or the eighth centuries, how many sins, up to that period, were remitted without the intervention of the Church! and what then happens to the dogma of the necessity of the sacrament of penance? . . . If there were no private penance and if the public absolution were supposed to forgive only the ecclesiastic

> penalty, then when and how did the conception of the remis-
> sion of the sin itself by the priest arise? . . . As for the classical
> theologians, they . . . accept a private absolution at the very
> moment of the imposition of the public penance. . . .[4]

Frequent auricular confession was such an important practice in Catholic pastoral teaching and spirituality after the
Council of Trent that theologians and even historians were unable to imagine that the Christians of the first centuries were
not subject to it. But minds have grown more sophisticated, as
one can see in the *Catechism of the Catholic Church,* paragraph
1447, where the "private" practice of penance is mentioned as
dating back only to the seventh century.

We must therefore avoid projecting back to the past more
recent preoccupations and usages. Not only the sacrament of
penance but also the eucharistic celebration is liable to the
same risk. Thus, the most common experience nowadays is
that of an assembly whose sole minister is the priest, standing
at the altar facing the people. But during the whole first millennium in the West (and it is still the case in the East), the
Eucharist was perceived as a common action which did not
place one celebrant facing the assembly, but united several
ministers and the assembly in an internal dialogue—through
the salutations and instructions—and in a communication
with the Lord, the only true high priest. The concern was not
to place the priest with either face or back to the people, but to
focus the attention of the whole assembly on its principal in-
terlocutor, who is God.

Let us mention an additional source of difficulty: the dissociation between exterior worship and interior prayer introduced into the Catholic way of thinking. In the West, when the
liturgy had become the business of clerics, celebrated in a
learned tongue unknown to the people, preachers developed
private devotions and exercises. Then worship was seen as an
external manifestation, a duty rendered to God and requiring
care for the appearances, such as baroque music, processions,
decorations, but not demanding too great a personal invest-
ment. Religious education stressed the individual relation to
God, to such a point that during solemn liturgical celebrations
one could see priests individually reciting their breviary, while

seated side by side in the sanctuary, and the faithful silently praying the rosary as their confessors had advised! In catechisms, worship was included in the chapter on moral obligations; it was regarded as the social form of the virtue of religion, that is, the fulfillment of the duties we have toward God.

In fact, Christian prayer, like Jewish prayer, is fundamentally the prayer of a people conscious of being God's people, and the liturgy is organized as the structured prayer of a community. In a historical study, one can give an account of liturgical institutions only by taking into consideration their communal destination.

Chapter 2

# Apostolic Times: The First Century

The transition from the Old to the New Covenant did not happen in an instant. It took several generations before the early Christian communities definitively broke away from ancient Israel and its cult. Thus, the Acts of the Apostles (21:28) relates how Paul still continued to come to the Temple; but he was accused of bringing along pagans who had been converted to Christ, a fact which caused his arrest in the year 58. In the same way, according to the wording of the canticle of Mary, the apostolic community regarded itself as belonging to the People of God (Luke 1:54-55) and was still hoping for the conversion of ancient Israel together with its institutions. The early Christian community did not take the initiative of separating itself from the Jewish community; on the contrary, it believed that from within this chosen people, it was welcoming the full realization of the "plan of the mystery hidden for ages in God" (Eph 3:9, and so forth) and ardently wished to communicate this revelation in order to obtain the conversion of Israel (Rom 11). It was official Judaism which decided to exclude the Nazorean's followers, whom it considered to belong to a sect gone astray.

After being rejected by the leaders of Israel, the first Christian communities developed their own institutions, under the guidance of the Holy Spirit. And the earliest Christian documents have preserved clues concerning the organization of their liturgical assemblies so that it is possible to reconstruct, at lest partially, what the celebrations of the apostolic age were like.

**The Sources**

The New Testament writings are the principal source for the study of the first Christian institutions. These writings allude to the celebrations of the early communities and contain some liturgical rulings. Their interpretation is sometimes uncertain, as is the case in particular for the Acts of the Apostles, which juxtaposes traditions of different times. Thus, in 6:1-7, exegetes have detected the traces of a twofold organization in the Jerusalem community: the Twelve retain the responsibility of the group called "Hebrews" (Hebrew- or Aramaic-speaking Jews converted to the Christian faith) whereas the Seven, instituted by the Apostles, are in charge of the "Hellenists" (Greek-speaking Jews converted to the Christian faith). This system of differentiated government must have disappeared soon in Jerusalem as a consequence of the persecution against the Hellenists, who were obliged to flee from the city (about 33–34), whereas the Twelve remained there (Acts 8:1). This twofold governance is scarcely explained in the text because at the time of the final redaction, about 75–80, it was disappearing: another organization was in the process of being established in the communities, with presbyters (elders) exercising the pastoral function of bishops (overseers) according to Acts 20:17, 28 and of deacons and bishops (overseers) according to Philippians 1:1.

The first Christian generations must have had to adapt to several new situations which affected the way the liturgy was conducted. Thus, with the destruction of the Jerusalem Temple in 70, they saw the definitive disappearance of the sacrificial worship of the Old Covenant. Then, they had to accept that, the return of Christ not being immediate, they had to set up institutions, both specific and stable, and see to the replacement of the apostles for the leadership of assemblies.

To the information supplied by the New Testament, we must add what we find in the church order of Syrian origin already mentioned above, the *Didache* or the *Teaching of the Twelve Apostles;* its final redaction seems to date back to the second century, but it contains older traditions. Concerning the liturgy, this work collected regulations on baptism, fasting, the Eucharist, and prayer (7.1–10.7), and especially two groups of blessings, one for the cup and the broken bread and one for after all have finished their meal (9–10).

Even though it seems copious, this documentation does not allow us to reconstruct all the liturgical institutions of the first century because we do not have complete descriptions but only allusions. Sometimes, Paul imparts more knowledge on the abuses he denounces than on the regular practice, for instance on the subject of Christian assemblies in Corinth. He had orally transmitted the norms while he was present in Corinth; when he decries the excesses committed during the Lord's supper, he simply refers to what he had previously taught without repeating it, or else he promises to return to settle things in person (1 Cor 11:34).

## The Assemblies or Synaxes

What characterizes the first Christian communities is their eagerness to gather together. Before Pentecost, it is Christ himself who appears as the Risen One to gather the group of his disciples and breathe into it his Spirit of resurrection: he transforms these disheartened and discouraged human beings, huddled behind the closed doors of their hiding place, into courageous preachers, confronting the leaders of their people. In these meetings, the risen Christ sets down the essential elements that constitute his Church: he converses with his disciples, he convinces them of his resurrection, he shares with them his Spirit and his word, he "breaks bread" and eats with them (Mark 16:14-20; Luke 24:13-53; John 20:19-29; Acts 1:3-8). Each manifestation of the Risen One ends with the sending into mission, which the gospels present under different modalities. Be it from a mountaintop in Galilee, this crossroad of pagan regions (Matt 28:16-20), or from Jerusalem, the light of the Nations (Luke 24:47), or during an overabundant catch of fish (John 21:1-14; cf. Luke 5:1-11 "catching people") or else at table (Mark 16:14-20), at each of his manifestations, the Risen One sends his disciples to proclaim the good news of the resurrection to the whole universe.

All these gestures and acts of the risen Christ are constitutive of the Christian assembly in its highest form, the Eucharist:

gathering together, recognizing the Risen One, proclaiming his word, breaking the bread and taking a meal, sending into mission. This last element is expressed under the form of an invocation in the oldest known eucharistic formula, that of the *Didache* (see p. 21):

> Let your Church be brought together from the ends of the earth into your Kingdom . . . (9.4).

> Gather it [the Church] 'together from the four winds.'. . . (10.5).[1]

After Pentecost, the narrative of the Acts presents a community knitted and fashioned by assemblies that seem to have been held daily. The first allusions to the Christian celebrations are found in the three "pictures" of the Jerusalem community: Acts 2:42-47; 4:32-35; 5:12-16. The chief characteristic is the communion *(koinonia)*, which is manifest in four domains: the apostles' teaching, the common ownership of goods, the breaking of the bread, and the prayers. When the disciples are to undertake actions and missions, these are decided in the community assemblies, and the community is immediately informed of the effects and results of such actions and missions (Acts 4:23); the same procedure will be observed in Antioch (Acts 13:2-3).

We are slightly better informed concerning the prayer of the community when it is afflicted with trials, in particular when Peter is arrested (with John), or kept in prison (Acts 4:23-31; 12:5, 12). On the former occasion, the story records the text of a prayer of thanksgiving (Acts 4:24-30).

The communities born outside Jerusalem as a result of missionary journeys were established in the same way, starting in assemblies formed around the preachers. Scattered allusions throughout the New Testament writings furnish some hints about those gatherings, for instance, on the way people prayed and prophesied in Corinth (1 Cor 11:2-12, 31; 14:40) and on the way Paul's letters were read during the synaxes (1 Thess 5:27). Likewise, the letters of the companions and successors of the apostles were destined to be read during the assemblies, as it is directed at the beginning or end of the documents, for example, in the Epistle to the Corinthians written by Clement of Rome and in the letters of Ignatius of Antioch.

## Meal of the Community and the "Lord's Supper"

In Acts, the first of the "pictures" mentioned above alludes to both common meals and the "breaking of the bread" (2:46). It is the manifestation of the risen Jesus which makes clear what we must understand by "breaking of the bread" (Luke 24:30-35; see also Acts 2:42; 20:7-22) and which elsewhere is called the "Lord's supper" (1 Cor 11:20).

There has been a great deal of discussion on the subject of the connection between common meal and eucharistic meal in apostolic times: In the beginning, was the Eucharist celebrated in the course of an "ordinary" meal? But must we ask the question in these terms? The fragments of information gathered in the New Testament do not permit us to recapture how the eucharistic assemblies of the first Christian communities were conducted. Besides, we must take into consideration their cultural context so different from our own, especially where meals are concerned.

According to the spirit of the Bible, all food must be seen as a gift from God. Every meal is accompanied by blessings through which the participants render thanks to God for food. Now, the bread evokes the word of God and the Law which cause us to live. "Remember . . . the LORD your God . . . [fed] you with manna with which neither you nor your ancestors were acquainted, in order to make you understand that one does not live by bread alone, but by every word that comes from the mouth of the LORD" (Deut 8:2-3; see also parallel passages whose references are found in most editions of the Bible). Wine and vine evoke God's solicitude for God's people and the happiness promised to them. Therefore, any meal is already an encounter, even a communion, with God.

Plutarch is credited with the saying, "The Greeks do not feel they have really dined if they have not dined with friends." In those societies, conviviality was more important than food and meals were the habitual place for communication. This is verified in the gospels, which often present Christ teaching on the occasion of a meal (for instance, Luke 7:36; 11:37; 14:1-24; and above all, the long farewell discourse in John 13–17). The modes of communion that a meal offers are many: sitting at the same table, sharing the same dish, the same food, exchanging thoughts and thinking alike. In Jewish society, specific religious rites are added to these modes of communion: the guests pray and bless God, sing psalms and recall God's wonders. In the beginning of our era, the Therapeutae, a fervent Jewish community, used to begin their meals with a commentary on sacred Scripture and a homily.

The *Didache* preserved Christian blessings composed according to this tradition:

> Now about the Eucharist: This is how to give thanks:
> First in connection with the cup:
>
> "We thank you, our Father, for the holy vine of David, your child. To you be glory forever."
>
> Then in connection with the piece [broken off the loaf]:
>
> "We thank you, our Father, for the life and knowledge which you have revealed through Jesus, your child. To you be glory forever.
>
> As this piece [of bread] was scattered over the hills and then was brought together and made one, so let your Church be brought together from the ends of the earth into your Kingdom. For yours is the glory and the power through Jesus Christ forever" (ch. 9).

In view of this, were the first Christian Eucharists celebrations joining an office of readings, similar to synagogue models, with the meal of a religious fellowship? Or else, were they community meals during which the presence and participation of the risen Christ were particularly stressed through the recalling of his teaching and salvific actions, above all the breaking of the bread?

The community meals were at once a realization and an expression of charity and mutual support, another aspect of communion in one single body. In times of want and famine, which did happen now and then as Acts 11:28 shows, the demands of mutual help led in all likelihood to the organization of daily meals for the benefit of the needy, and this was perhaps one cause of the progressive dissociation between community meals and the exclusively eucharistic meal. The letter of Jude (v. 12) already alludes to community meals without Eucharist and calls them "love-feasts."

## The "Lord's Supper" at Corinth

Paul's first letter to the Corinthians is one of the better documented sources on the liturgical traditions of apostolic times. However, because it is made up chiefly of remonstrances, the letter gives more information on the abuses committed by the Christians of Corinth than on the regular practices of that church. This is the case concerning the "Lord's supper" in particular (11:17-34).

The apostle's reproaches are directed at the Corinthians' reprehensible behavior because their selfishness at the table of the community meal is incompatible with the "Lord's supper" since the latter unites them into one single body. But the brevity of this passage does not allow us to know what the relationship was between the community meal and the ritual of the Last Supper, whose tradition Paul recalls.

Were the difficulties that arose in Corinth peculiar to that community? Were they due to the particularities of the culture in which these Christians lived, for they came mainly from paganism and were not acquainted with the tradition of the Jewish religious meals? Were those Corinthians still too strongly influenced by the pagan cultic practices, the sacred meals, and the consumption of food offered to idols (1 Cor 8) to discern the newness of the "Lord's supper" and its paschal dimension as the pledge of resurrection? All these are open questions which we lack the means to answer. What is evident in any case is the difficulty encountered by the first missionaries when they undertook to initiate converts from pagan milieus to the Eucharist.

## The Places Used for the Assemblies

The Acts of the Apostles (20:7-12) recount a gathering in Troas (Asia Minor) during which Paul bid farewell to the local community. The breaking of the bread and the discussions held by the apostle are mentioned. The meeting took place on the third floor of a building and this detail allows us to evaluate the number of the participants: one thinks of no more than a score of persons.

In general, accounts suggest that the meetings took place in private houses: Acts 2:46; 5:42; 20:20. When the apostles and their companions were still able to take part in the Jewish liturgy, they needed to gather by themselves, in their own houses, for everything that was particular to them and presupposed faith in the risen Christ. Several of these houses are designated in a more precise manner: in Jerusalem, "the room upstairs" (Acts 1:13) and "the house of Mary, the mother of John whose other name was Mark" (Acts 12:12); the houses of Lydia in Philippi (Acts 16:15, 40), Prisca and Aquila in Ephesus (Rom 16:5; 1 Cor 16:19), and Nympha in Laodicea (Col 4:15). Philemon also welcomed meetings in his house (Phlm 2). In these letters, we find again and again the same formula, "the church in your, (her, their) house."

According to the story in Acts 1:15, one hundred and twenty persons were assembled in the "room upstairs" when time came to see to the replacement of Judas. This symbolic number is required by the narrative since it is describing an act constitutive of the new people of God; it is a reference to the twelve tribes (twelve times ten, a basic element in the organization of the people). With the exception of this mention, there is no number given concerning the size of the gatherings in houses. But the usual dimensions of these buildings did not allow for a group larger than twenty or thirty persons.

### The Accounts of Baptisms

The Acts of the Apostles speak of numerous baptisms: the three thousand converted on the day of Pentecost (2:14-41), the Samaritans after Philip's preaching (8:4-25), the Ethiopian eunuch (8:26-40), Saul (Acts 9:10-19), the centurion Cornelius and his household (10:44-48), Lydia and her household during a mission of Paul (16:13-14), the jailer and his family in Philippi after he took care of Paul and Silas (16:32-33), and so forth. However, a certain diversity in the practices is notice-able: Cornelius and his household are baptized after an out-pouring of the Holy Spirit at a new Pentecost (10:44-48). The Samaritans, on the other hand, first receive baptism in the name of the Lord Jesus after the proclamation of the good news by Philip (8:12, 16), and some time later, Peter and John lay their hands on them for the gift of the Holy Spirit (8:17). The Johannites of Ephesus first receive John's baptism; after-wards they are baptized in the name of the Lord Jesus; then Paul lays his hands on them and the Holy Spirit comes down on them (19:1-7).

**The Baptismal Rite.** Among all these stories, the only one that describes the baptismal rite is that of the Ethiopian's con-version: "Both of them, Philip and the eunuch, went down into the water, and Philip baptized him." To the request for baptism, some manuscripts add a profession of faith on the part of the Ethiopian: "Philip said, 'If you believe with all your heart, it is permissible.' The eunuch answered, 'I believe that Jesus Christ is the Son of God.'" The practice of baptism by im-mersion is confirmed by Paul's preaching, which compares the descent into the water and the coming out of it to the bur-ial into death and the resurrection of Jesus (Rom 6:1-23).

Elsewhere, the reception of baptism is mentioned in the passive form, "they were baptized," without further allusion to the rite and without any naming of the baptizers. In the sto-ries of Paul's conversion, it is said that Ananias laid his hand on Saul but it is not said specifically that he administered bap-tism (9:18; 22:16). Later on, Peter gives the order to baptize Cornelius and his household (10:48). As for Paul, he reminds the Corinthians that very few among them have been baptized by him (1 Cor 1:14-17). Despite their brevity, these accounts are sufficient to show the distinction between Christian baptism and Jewish ablutions, self-administered, as a sign of penance and purification: Christian baptism is received; one does not baptize oneself.

**The Baptismal Preparation.** The preparation for baptism is but briefly touched upon. The Ethiopian had the benefit of only a short instruction from the deacon Philip and was immediately baptized, but he was well prepared since he was used to reading the Bible rather than a commentary (Acts 8:26-39). The instruction of Apollos was longer: this fervent Jew, well-versed in the Scriptures, "had been instructed in the Way of the Lord . . . and taught accurately the things concerning Jesus," but he knew only the baptism of John; his instruction was completed by Priscilla and Aquila (Acts 18:24-26).

The conciseness of these accounts does not permit us to assess the duration of the instruction preparing the candidates for baptism. The purpose of the writers is not historical but theological, to make manifest the action of the Holy Spirit in the growth of the Church; the detailed description of institutions was not part of their plans. We also notice that most candidates came from Judaism, either directly or from the ranks of the proselytes and "those who feared God"; therefore, they had already been prepared through their knowledge of the Scriptures.

**The Order of Baptism in the *Didache*.** The *Didache* gives us more information on the teaching preparatory to baptism (7.1), since it supplies one of the elements of this preparatory teaching, the treatise of the two ways (chs. 1–6). We have here a tradition that has its origin in the Bible, transposed into Christian catechesis. The way of life leads to God and consists in the observance of the commandments, but the practice of evil is the way of death and leads away from God (see Deut 30:15-20; Matt 7:13-14, the two gates). This catechesis confronted the candidate for baptism with a decisive option: conversion concerns the whole life of a person, for behavior is the visible criterion that shows whether one belongs to the way of life or the way of death.

As for the baptismal ritual itself, the *Didache* treats only the disputed questions: the quality of the water, the lack of water, and fasting:

> Now about baptism: this is how to baptize. Give public instruction on all these points, and then "baptize" in running water, "in the name of the Father and of the Son and of the Holy Spirit." If you do not have running water, baptize in some other. If you cannot in cold, then in warm. If you have neither,

then pour water on the head three times "in the name of the Father, Son, and Holy Spirit." Before the baptism, moreover, the one who baptizes and the one being baptized must fast, and any other who can. And you must tell the one being baptized to fast for one or two days beforehand (7.1-4).

The prescriptions on the quality of the water are probably answers to Christians who had come from Judaism, because Jewish theologians distinguished up to six different degrees of purity, from the stagnant water of cisterns to the running water welling up from springs, and in certain cases there was an obligation to use running water. The *Didache* recognizes the superior value of running water for the baptismal immersion but does not impose it as a necessary condition. These distinctions, which will not be found in subsequent periods, suggest that special installations for baptizing were not yet available and it was therefore indispensable to make provisions for different situations.

The regulations of the *Didache* also foresee the case in which immersion is impossible for lack of water and prescribes baptism by pouring water three times on the candidate's head. In both cases, the same trinitarian baptismal formula is used, according to the final words of Matthew's gospel (28:19).

The last prescription of this order of baptism is the fast preceding baptism. It concerns the baptizer, the candidate, and "others" whose identities are not spelled out.

## The Liturgy in Time

The young Church manifested, sometimes forcefully, its difference from Judaism. Still, the fact is that Jewish institutions have actually been the crucible and womb of Christian institutions. Thus, Israel and the Church live the Covenant according to the rhythm of the week with each observing one pivotal day. From now on, for Christians, this day is Sunday, which the risen Christ has pointed out to the group of the apostles as the "day of the Lord"—first day of the week and new anchor of the weekly rhythm—replacing the sabbath. "When it was evening on that day, the first day of the week,

. . . Jesus came. . . . A week later . . . Jesus came . . ." (John 20:19, 26).

Thus, since the Lord's resurrection, Christian communities meet every Sunday. The Acts of the Apostles mentions the fact when speaking of Paul's visit to Troas (20:7), and the he himself mentions it in relation to a collection of solidarity (1 Cor 16:2). The *Didache* follows suit, "On every Lord's Day—his special day—come together and break bread and give thanks . . ." (ch. 14). The same church order also picks out the two days of weekly fast, Wednesday and Friday, and mandates praying the Our Father three times a day (ch. 8). These rhythms—whether weekly or daily—derive from Jewish practices.

The regularity of the Christian assemblies in the West was recognized by pagans as a characteristic trait at a time when the surrounding society lived according to the rhythm of a monthly calendar and of feasts that recurred irregularly; only in the East was the week observed. We hear an echo of this in a letter of Pliny the Younger, the governor of Bithynia (to the north of the present-day capital of Turkey), sent to the Emperor Trajan in 112. The purpose of the letter is vague precisely because it was written by an outside observer who knew Christians only through denunciations and prosecutions brought against them. He had questioned apostates:

> They also declared that the sum total of their guilt or error amounted to no more than this: they had met regularly before dawn on a fixed day to chant verses alternately amongst themselves in honor of Christ as if to a god. . . . After this ceremony, it had been their custom to disperse and reassemble later to take food of an ordinary, harmless kind; but they had in fact given up this practice since my edict, issued on your instructions, which banned all political societies.[2]

In the phrase "they had met on a fixed day," we may see an allusion to Sunday, but also to the other days of meetings during the week, Wednesday and Friday. Pliny also mentions meetings held at dawn, and others, in the evening, which Christians discontinued after the imperial power had forbidden night meetings—a measure of political security. One can see in this passage an allusion to prayer meetings and to the Eucharist.

In fact, the disciples of the Risen One "devoted themselves to . . . the prayers" (Acts 2:42-47). However, we do not know much about the organization of their daily praise. It is true that treatises on Christian prayer, written later, recognize in apostolic practices the origin of the three times of daily prayer: the gathering of the apostles at the third hour (9:00 a.m.) on the day of Pentecost, Peter's prayer on the roof at the sixth hour (noon), and the ascent of Peter and John to the Temple for prayer at the ninth hour (3:00 p.m.) according to Acts 2:1, 15; 10:9; 3:1. The treatises also added the praise of Paul and Silas at midnight in prison, according to Acts 16:25. But these narratives in Acts do not explicitly speak of daily Christian meetings at these different hours.

According to Acts 2:46 and 3:1, the apostolic community frequented the Temple with assiduity—for instance, Peter and John at the time of the evening sacrifice—but no information is given on the daily praise of the Christian communities after their exclusion from official Judaism and then, later on, after the destruction of the Temple. This last event was to have important repercussions on the consciousness of the young Church. Ancient Israel offered God daily sacrifices of praise in the name of humankind: this was its priestly function. But the destruction of the Temple prevented Israel from performing this liturgy. Did the young Church become aware at that time that from then on it fell to its lot to ensure this priestly ministry in the Sunday liturgy? This could be suggested by the fact that the *Didache* (14.2) appropriates Malachi's prophecy (1:11, 14) on the sacrifice of praise.

We know next to nothing about the participation of the first Christian communities in the yearly Jewish feasts. We are told that Paul, at the time of his meeting in Miletus with the elders of Ephesus (Acts 20:16), was eager to be in Jerusalem for the day of Pentecost in the year 58. On the other hand, in his letters, Paul clearly affirms the originality of the Christian Pasch (for instance in 1 Cor 5:7-8).

## The Liturgical Ministries

In the New Testament and the *Didache*, we discern several forms and stages in the evolution of Christian ministries.

Among these, some corresponded to the missionary movement, to wit, apostles, prophets, and teachers, and others were evolving toward a hierarchy with three degrees, overseers (bishops), presbyters (priests), and deacons. The varied names derive from the practices of the different cultural groups, Palestinian Jews and Hellenists, and the services needed in the communities, teaching, mission, government, service at table.

However, no allusion is ever made to the liturgical functions of these ministries, and how the meetings were conducted is known to us only from Paul's instructions to the community at Corinth: he speaks of the way in which speech should be used in the assemblies and gives it to be understood that anybody present, whether man or woman, is free to pray and prophesy (1 Cor 11-12). But the more specific function of presiding over the celebrations, a question which has been such a prominent preoccupation in the churches for a few centuries, is never mentioned in the New Testament, probably because it caused no difficulty:

> Now about the apostles and prophets: Act in line with the gospel precept. Welcome every apostle on arriving, as if he were the Lord. But he must not stay beyond one day. In case of necessity, the next day too. If he stays three days, he is a false prophet . . . (*Didache* 11.3).

> You must, then, elect for yourselves bishops and deacons who are a credit to the Lord, men who are gentle, generous, faithful, and well tried. For their ministry to you is identical with that of the prophets and teachers. . . . (*Didache* 15.1).[3]

### The Rites of the Apostolic Church

Besides the breaking of the bread, or Lord's supper, and baptism, the New Testament writings allude to other rites, but few in number. What we mostly hear of is the laying on of hands, practiced either for the gift of the Spirit in connection with baptism (Acts 8:15-17) or for healing of the sick (Acts 9:12, 17; 28:8) or for sending into mission for the service of the community (Acts 6:6; 13:1-3; 1 Tim 4:14; 5:22; 2 Tim 1:6).

The practice of anointing the sick with oil is mentioned in connection with the mission of the Twelve (Mark 6:13). It is described in the Letter of James (5:14-16): the persons who visit the sick are not miracle-workers who had received the gift of healing (1 Cor 12:9 and so forth) but members of the collegial leadership of the community. This passage is also the only one that mentions the forgiveness of sins committed after baptism, whose pardon is shown here as a consequence of the anointing with oil; the other allusions to the forgiveness of sin in the New Testament refer to baptism.

Chapter 3

# The Liturgy in Christian Minorities during Times of Relative Clandestinity

In the evolution of liturgical institutions, it is important to make a separate study of the second and third centuries. Indeed, this period is distinct from apostolic times because the apostles were no longer alive and were of necessity replaced in the leadership of Christian communities. Besides, momentous events had modified the status of the young Church: its rejection by Israel and the destruction of the Temple. The eschatological expectations had also changed since the communities no longer counted on an imminent return of the Lord and as a consequence were setting up the institutions they needed to live for an extended period of time.

But those Christian communities established in cities found themselves in a precarious situation because their religion did not enjoy official status in the Empire. They were subjected to accusations and calumnies, and even endured several waves of persecution before the Edict of Toleration in 313 recognized the freedom of religion.

As had been the case for Diaspora Judaism, Christian communities of this period were established chiefly in the cities around the Mediterranean basin, subject to the power of the Roman Empire. Therefore, they shared the same culture and enjoyed communications that were relatively easy for the time, especially by sea routes. The Roman Empire was not yet administratively divided into Eastern Empire and Western Empire, but was a unified entity further strengthened by the use of one language, Greek. The Hebrew Scriptures (which we call the Old Testament) had already been translated into Greek when the first Christian missionaries began to preach.

As regards their interior organization, Christian communities developed in a certain autonomy. Guided, of course, by the common traditions originating with the apostles and led by the Holy Spirit, in each city they gave themselves the different institutions necessary for their functioning. Centralizing currents appeared only later, after the ordeal of persecutions. From one community to the next, circumstances varied according to the size of cities, the Christians' settling in one or several neighborhoods, the proximity of Jewish communities, the social and cultural origin of the members, and so forth.

After being rejected by official Judaism, Christian communities turned to the pagans. But such a recruitment made it necessary to provide a more thorough teaching for the new members, and especially instruction in the Bible. These new converts were imbued with a religious and philosophical culture often very sophisticated but foreign to biblical categories. In order to assume this new mission, certain Christian communities created and developed catechetical schools, like the one in Alexandria under Origen's direction in the first half of the third century.

The establishment of institutions occurred progressively and not without travail, sometimes in a groping manner. It was necessary to find authentically Christian ways in the midst of the deviations of Gnostic and other groups. This is visible in the gradual formation of the canon of the Scriptures and the organization of ministries. All this influenced the tenor of the synaxes and the manner of celebration.

### The Sources

Written documentation is already more important than in apostolic times. In the first Christian writers, it is possible to glean some allusions to liturgical institutions and even, here and there, more systematic descriptions. Thus, in his correspondence, Cyprian, bishop of Carthage (d. 258), gives us information on the way in which he created or modified certain institutions. Tertullian (in 211) allows us a glimpse when in a discussion on the importance of oral tradition he indicates the part it has in the liturgy:

> Thus . . . when we are just about to enter the water, at that moment and also somewhat earlier in church, bowed under the presider's hand, we solemnly affirm that we renounce the devil and its pomp and its angels. After this, we are immersed three times while we recite answers somewhat fuller than our Lord established in the gospel. Then, straightening up, we sip, as firstfruits, a mixture of milk and honey, and beginning with that day we abstain from our daily bath for a whole week. The sacrament of the Eucharist, prescribed for all by the Lord at the time of the supper, we also receive during the pre-dawn meetings, and from the very hands of those who preside over the assembly. We make the offerings for the dead on the anniversary day of their "birth." On the day of the Lord, we hold fasting or praying on our knees as forbidden. We enjoy the same dispensation from Easter to Pentecost. The possibility of letting a little of either our cup or our bread fall to the ground makes us painfully anxious. Each time we set out, take a forward step, enter or exit, put on clothes or shoes, go to the baths or to the dining room, light a lamp, go to bed, sit down, in a word with every movement required by our way of living, we mark our forehead with a sign [of the cross] (*De corona* 3-4).[1]

**The Church Order Known as the "Apostolic Tradition."** Some elements of ritual and liturgical prayer have also come down to us through church orders. We are referring especially to an anonymous collection which certain historians around 1910 thought they could call *Apostolic Tradition* and which they attributed to Hippolytus of Rome (ca. 170–ca. 236).[2] This title was read on the pedestal of a statue found and restored during the Renaissance (1551); for a long time, it was believed that the statue represented Hippolytus, but a more recent, more credible hypothesis holds that it is a personalization of Philosophy.

The document has reached us in a defective state: the Greek original has been lost, and the oldest translation—into Latin—made at the end of the fifth century, is mutilated. A few, more recent translations (dating from the eleventh to the nineteenth centuries) into Coptic, Arabic, and Geez (Ethiopic), have preserved a more complete text which, in one case or the other, seems integral; however, some divergences exist between these versions.

As to the redaction of this document, which is a collection of rulings, we shall benefit by a comparison with legislative codes in general. It is well known that laws and codes do not bear the names of those who transcribed them, but the names of the personalities who promulgated them. Similarly, the church orders are anonymous writings, and the names they eventually receive designate either the compilers who gathered them or the authorities who imposed them, not to speak of late attributions due to some absentminded copyist.

In the *Apostolic Tradition*, no indication betrays either the redactor or a specifically Roman origin. Now, Hippolytus of Rome is the author of important theological treatises, not of legislative collections. Moreover, his ecclesiastical career would not have earned him any authority in matters of discipline; the contrary is more plausible. In fact, this Roman presbyter quarreled with Pope Zephyrinus (199–217) and was opposed to his successor, Callistus (217–222), to the point of heading a rival community. Later on, he was exiled to Sardinia with Pope Pontian, and martyrdom obtained for him his reintegration into the Church.

Analysis of the document suggests a date somewhere in the first half of the third century and a Syrian or Alexandrian origin. It has been inserted in several other church orders or altered in derivative documents. It is difficult to determine what kind of community it was intended for. When treating of the baptismal liturgy, it mentions numerous ministers, which supposes a rather important church; but elsewhere, the community seems small since the bishop can distribute Communion by himself (ch. 22, obscure text) and visit all the sick (ch. 34).

The contents of this document show that at this time of oral tradition, it seemed useful to collect the regulations concerning certain liturgical institutions since it treats in succession the subjects of ordination, Eucharist, baptism, synaxes, and prayer.

Among the ministries and states of life it enumerates, the *Apostolic Tradition* specifies that only three ordinations include the laying on of hands, those of bishop, presbyter, and deacon.

For these ordinations, it supplies elements of ritual as well as the formulas in use (chs. 2–14). The ritual for the ordination of the bishop is presented within its liturgical framework, that is the Sunday eucharistic synaxis; one element of the formulary is given in full, that of the Eucharistic Prayer of chapter 4, itself followed by the blessings for the offerings of oil, milk products, and olives (chs. 5 and 6).

The second section, rather lengthy (chs. 15–21), deals with baptism: the examination of candidates, catechumenate, celebration of baptism, and Eucharist of neophytes. Then, without transition, one reads rulings concerning regular communal practices (evening liturgy, common meal, hours of prayer, fasting, ministers' duties) and home practices (spouses' prayer, sign of the cross).

***Didascalia Apostolorum* (The Catholic Teaching of the Twelve Apostles).** Here again, we have a church order, but the part on the liturgy is less prominent than in the preceding document. This book contains chiefly pastoral exhortations addressed to bishops concerning the exercise of their ministry. The organization of the synaxes, the welcome given to strangers, the paschal celebrations, the calendar, and the fasts in preparation for Easter are discussed. The reconciliation of sinners also holds a large place in this document; mercy is emphasized, but there is no description of the liturgical aspects of the service.

This work was written in Greek, but the original has been lost. The text has come down to us in translations, in particular in Syriac and Latin. It goes back to the first half of the third century and seems to have originated in the region of Antioch in Syria.[3]

### The Assemblies

While the exercise of legally recognized religions in the Roman Empire was public and was manifested by buildings, monuments, and official cults, Christian communities existed only in their assemblies. Threatened as they were, they could not open their doors to all comers; they had to control the entrances and sometimes even hold their meetings in secret. Preachers, pastors, and writers stressed the importance of these assemblies and urged Christians to attend them. Among many others, here are three voices. First, Ignatius of Antioch:

> [Those] who fail to join in your worship show [their] arrogance. . . . Try to gather more frequently to celebrate God's Eucharist and to praise [God] (*Letter to the Ephesians* 5.3; 13.1).

> Run off—all of you—to one temple of God, as it were, to one altar, to one Jesus Christ (*Letter to the Magnesians* 7.2).

> Flee, then, the wicked tricks and snares of the prince of this world. . . . Rather, meet together, all of you, with a single heart (*Letter to the Philadelphians* 6.2).[4]

Then, Justin in about 152:

> And on the day called Sunday there is a meeting in one place of those who live in cities or the country, and the memoirs of the apostles or the writings of the prophets are read as long as time permits. . . . We all hold this common gathering on Sunday, since it is the first day, on which God transforming darkness and matter made the universe, and Jesus Christ our Saviour rose from the dead on the same day. For they crucified him on the day before Saturday, and on the day after Saturday, he appeared to his apostles and disciples and taught them these things which I have passed on to you also for your serious consideration (*First Apology* 67.3, 8).[5]

And last, the *Didascalia*:

> You, however, the bishops, . . . in your congregations in the holy churches hold your assemblies (in accordance with) all good manners . . . (12,130).
> Now when you teach, again command and warn the people to persevere in the assembly of the church, and not to be stopped but constantly to be assembled that no one diminish the church by not assembling, and cause the body of Christ to be smaller by a member. . . . Since now you are the members of Christ, do not scatter yourselves from the church by not assembling. . . . Deprive not our Saviour of his members. . . . Make not your affairs of the world of more account than the word of God. But on the Lord's day leave everything and run eagerly to your church. . . . If not, what excuse have they as over against those who before God do not assemble on the

Lord's day to hear the word of life and be nourished with the divine food which abides for ever? (13,135-136)

Thus, endeavor never to withdraw yourself from the assembly of the church . . . (13,137).

Be steadfast therefore and assemble with the faithful, with those who are being saved in your mother the church, she who lives and is vivifying (13,138).

In these three testimonies, the focus is on the Sunday assemblies. But elsewhere, there are allusions to weekday meetings.

## The Places Used for the Assemblies

For the second and third centuries, archeological data are rare. Christian monuments dating back to that period have been so thoroughly remodeled, especially by being enlarged, that their original state is very difficult to rediscover. However, the vestiges of a house-church were found under the desert sand in eastern Syria at Dura-Europos, a city that was an ancient military Roman colony on the Euphrates and was never rebuilt. The house, which had been modified to be used for Christian gatherings in 232, was destroyed with the city in 265. Similar to neighboring dwellings, it contained several rooms: one of them on the ground floor, measuring about 39 feet by 16 feet, could accommodate a group of thirty to fifty persons; another room was equipped for baptisms.

Other pieces of information come to us from written sources, in particular Eusebius of Caesarea (265–340). In the *Ecclesiastical History*,[6] he describes the development of communities and the construction of buildings during the period of religious peace that followed the edict of Gallienus in 260, then the destruction caused by the persecution of Diocletian, beginning in 303:

It was possible to see of what favor the rulers in each church were thought worthy by all the procurators and governors. And how could anyone describe those assemblies attended by thousands, and the multitude of the gatherings in every city, and the glorious concourses in the houses of prayer, because of which, not being satisfied any longer with the ancient buildings,

they built, from the foundations up, spacious churches . . .
(8.1).

> We saw with our own eyes the houses of prayer cast down
> to the very foundations from top to bottom, and the inspired
> and sacred Scriptures given over to flames in the midst of the
> market places (8.2).

Eusebius still uses the expression "houses of prayer," but
he also applies to them the word "church," which at first designated the gathering, the people convoked by God. The practice of the communities in these precarious situations also
shows that Christian worship was not linked to an edifice or
to a specific locale; this is what differentiated Christianity at
the time from other religions, whose cults were connected to
temples. The place where Christians assembled for the
synaxes was not the dwelling of a divinity, as were the temples, but the house of the assembly, as were (and are) the synagogues. The conviction, inherited from Judaism, that Christian
communities have of being a people of God corroborates this.
In contradistinction, pagan religions did not share this conviction, but hoped to extend the protection of the god or goddess
over the whole city.

The modest size of the locales first used by Christian communities did not allow large gatherings. How did people man-
age in big cities like Rome? Through a document preserved by
Eusebius in the *Ecclesiastical History*, we know for a fact that at
the time of Pope Cornelius, in 251, the Christians of the imperial capital were already numerous. This document is a list of
those who are the beneficiaries of the offerings, that is, the
clergy and the poor.

> One bishop . . . forty-six presbyters, seven deacons, seven sub-
> deacons, fifty-two exorcists, readers together with doorkeep-
> ers, more than fifteen hundred widows with persons in
> distress, all of whom the grace and kindness of the Master sup-
> ported (6.43).

Basing themselves on these figures, historians estimate the
number of Christians at between 10,000 and 30,000. Such numbers suggest a multitude of small groupings in the neighborhoods where Christians lived. We also know that certain of

these neighborhood communities were made up of "immigrants," natives of the eastern provinces who had settled in the capital. Some of these ethnic groups continued to observe the traditions of their places of origin, which provoked some conflicts, especially with Pope Victor in 190 concerning Paschal celebrations.

The enlargement of the places of assembly led to the regulation of their arrangement, as we can read in the *Didascalia* (12,130-131).

> But in your congregations in the holy churches hold your assemblies in (accordance with) all good manners, and fashion the places for the [brothers and sisters] carefully in sobriety. And for the presbyters let there be separated a place on the eastern side of the house, and let the bishop's chair be among them and let the presbyters sit with him.
>
> And again, let the [laypeople] sit in another eastern part of the house. For thus is it required that the presbyters shall sit in the eastern part of the house with the bishops, and afterwards the laymen, and then the women; so that when you stand up to pray, the leaders may stand first, and after them the laymen, and then also the women.
>
> Indeed, it is required that you pray toward the east, as knowing that which is written: "Give glory to God, who rides upon the heaven of heavens toward the east" (Ps 67[68]:33).

## The Eucharistic Celebration

The oldest description of the eucharistic celebration is in the *First Apology* of St. Justin. In this work, the author wants to refute the calumnies spread abroad on the subject of Christian meetings and to explain, in a language accessible to all, the eucharistic celebrations and baptisms that formed a part of these assemblies.

> We, however, after thus washing the one who has been convinced and signified . . . assent, lead [this one] to those who are called [brothers and sisters], where they are assembled. Then, they earnestly offer common prayers for themselves and the one who has been illuminated and all others everywhere. . . . On finishing the prayers we greet each other with a kiss. Then bread and a cup of water and mixed wine are brought to the

president of the [brothers and sisters] and he, taking them,
sends up praise and glory to the Father of the universe through
the name of the Son and of the Holy Spirit, and offers thanksgiving at some length that we have been deemed worthy to receive these things from [the Father]. When he has finished the
prayers and the thanksgiving, the whole congregation present
assents, saying, "Amen." . . . Those whom we call deacons
give to each of those present a portion of the consecrated bread
and wine and water, and they take it to the absent.

And on the day called Sunday there is a meeting in one
place of those who live in cities or the country, and the mem-
oirs of the apostles or the writings of the prophets are read as
long as time permits. When the reader has finished, the president in a discourse urges and invites [us] to the imitation of
these noble things. Then we all stand up together and offer
prayers. And, as said before, when we have finished the prayer,
bread is brought, and wine and water, and the president similarly sends up prayers and thanksgivings to the best of his abil-
ity, and the congregation assents, saying the Amen; the
distribution, and reception of the consecrated [elements] . . .
takes place and [the consecrated elements] are sent to the absent by the deacons. Those who prosper, and who so wish, con-
tribute, . . . as much as [they] choose to. What is collected is
deposited with the president, and he takes care of orphans and
widows . . . briefly, he is the protector of all those in need
(65.67).

We recognize in this testimony the organization of the eucharistic celebration as it was henceforth transmitted, with the
following elements in this order: the Liturgy of the Word, with
readings and preaching; general intercessions; the kiss of
peace and the preparation of the bread and wine; the
Eucharistic Prayer, with the Amen of the assembly (which is
said standing); Communion, which is also sent to the absent.

The kiss of peace follows the general intercessions, a position on which all the documents before the fifth century agree,
in the East as well as in the West. After this date the kiss of
peace became a part of the communion rites in Rome and
North Africa.

Justin connects all the aspects of ecclesial communion to the
Christian assembly: prayers, eucharistic Communion, sharing,

organized help for the needy. He does not omit mentioning
that the baptized consider themselves "brothers" (and sisters).
But he does not make any allusion to a community meal.

No clear testimony has come down to us on the subject of
this mutation of the eucharistic celebration, whose model, the
Last Supper, was indubitably a fellowship meal. Several evolutions probably converged. We think first of the material conditions: the increase in the size of congregations must have
burst the too narrow framework of the community meal. But
also, very early, theological reflection certainly influenced the
perception that the faithful may have had of the "Lord's
Supper" and had an effect on liturgical development.

Thus, the experiences of religious meals and sacred meals
may have influenced the understanding of the "Lord's Supper."
According to a concept proper to Judaism, this meal was first
seen as "eating with Christ" recognized as present through
faith, as shown by the testimony of the disciples at Emmaus.
An evolution occurred in the direction of "eating Christ" according to the concept of Jewish sacrifices ("partners in the
altar," 1 Cor 10:18) and pagan sacred meals, in which the obla-
tions offered to the deity and accepted by it were regarded as
bearers of its presence (see what is said of the food offered to
idols in 1 Cor 8–10).

In the same way, the development made in the understanding of the mystery of Christ and of all that is implied in
his divinity, was bound to give rise to new forms of liturgical
expression inspired by the surrounding culture and the ways
it manifested its piety and veneration. This development is already perceptible in the titles given to Christ: the servant of
God, (according to Isaiah 42 and so forth), proclaimed in the
Acts of the Apostles (for instance 3:13, 26; 4:27), the *Didache*,
and the *Apostolic Tradition*; the Logos (Word or Reason),
Shepherd, Teacher, true and unique High Priest, later recognized by Christian communities.

The *Apostolic Tradition* brings us some information on the
ritual of Communion and the respect owed the eucharistic
gifts. But what is still more interesting is that it has preserved
in chapter 4 the text of a Eucharistic Prayer in the ritual of the
ordination of a bishop. The Greek text having been lost, we

stumble against a few difficulties which we will indicate as the occasion arises.

[1] And when he has been made bishop, all shall offer the kiss of peace, greeting him because he has been made worthy. Then the deacons shall present the offering to him; and he, laying his hands on it with all the presbytery, shall give thanks, saying:
[2] The Lord be with you;

and all shall say:
And with your spirit.
Up with your hearts.
We have them with the Lord.
Let us give thanks to the Lord.
It is fitting and right.

And then he shall continue thus:
[3] We render thanks to you, O God, through your beloved child Jesus Christ, whom in the last times you sent to us as savior and redeemer and angel of your will; who is your inseparable Word through whom you made all things, and in whom you were well pleased. You sent him from heaven into the Virgin's womb; and, conceived in the womb, he was made flesh and was manifested as your Son, being born of the holy Spirit and the Virgin. Fulfilling your will and gaining for you a holy people, he stretched out his hands when he should suffer, that he might release from suffering those who have believed in you.
[4] And when he was betrayed to voluntary suffering that he might destroy death, and break the bonds of the devil, and tread down hell, and shine upon the righteous, and fix a term, and manifest the resurrection, he took bread and gave thanks to you, saying, 'Take, eat; this is my body, which shall be broken for you.' Likewise also the cup, saying, 'This is my blood, which is shed for you; when you do this, you make my remembrance.'
[5] Remembering therefore his death and resurrection, we offer to you the bread and the cup, giving you thanks because you have held us worthy to stand before you and minister to you.
[6] And we ask that you would send your holy Spirit upon the offering of your holy Church; that gathering [it] into one, you would grant to all who partake of the holy things (to partake) for the fullness of the holy Spirit for the strengthening of faith in truth, that we may praise and glorify you through your child

Jesus Christ, [7] through whom be glory and honour to you, with the holy Spirit, in your holy church, both now and to the ages of ages. Amen (ch. 4).

We do not know whether this formulary is complete or we have only the main lines of a Eucharistic Prayer that the celebrant was at liberty to develop. But the structure underlying all the Eucharistic Prayers that were to come later is found in this passage. (The numbers refer to those placed in square brackets above.)

- the initial dialogue (2);
- an introductory formula expressing thanksgiving and an anamnesis (recalling) of the work of salvation accomplished by Christ, ending with the narrative of the eucharistic institution (3-4);
- a formula of offering, introduced by a paschal anamnesis and followed by a second formula of thanksgiving (5);
- an epiclesis (calling down) of the Holy Spirit on the offerings of the assembly, with the mention of praise (6);
- a trinitarian doxology (7).

We have here a unified composition, whereas the eucharistic formulary of the *Didache* is made up of a series of blessings (see p. 21). However, the *Didascalia*, a document contemporary with the *Didache*, seems to allude to a formulary that two celebrants would use together. On the occasion of the local bishop's welcoming a visiting bishop, it says, "When you offer the oblation, let him speak. But if he is wise and gives the honor to you, and does not wish to offer, yet let him speak over the cup" (12,133). A formulary made up of several blessings, as in the *Didache*, easily lent itself to a proclamation by several voices.

These scant allusions are the rare testimonies we know concerning this evolution of the eucharistic formulary, consisting at first of a series of blessings *(Didache)* and developed at a later date into a composition all of one piece, unifying all the elements of the previous blessings.

## The Synaxes on Weekdays

For the period of the second and third centuries, we lack any precise data on the occurrence of synaxes on weekdays. The practices must have varied depending on local traditions and the possibility of meeting, limited in times of persecutions and regular during peaceful periods. On this subject, we turn once more to the *Apostolic Tradition* (chs. 25–40) for the most abundant information, whose interpretation however is uncertain. We read of evening meetings, charity meals, and morning gatherings during which teaching was imparted:

> When the bishop is present, and evening has come, a deacon brings in a lamp; and standing in the midst of all the faithful who are present, (the bishop) shall give thanks. . . .

> We give you thanks, Lord, through your Son Jesus Christ our Lord, through whom you have shone upon us and revealed to us the inextinguishable light. So when we have completed the length of the day and have come to the beginning of the night, and have satisfied ourselves with the light of day which you created for our satisfying; and since now through your grace we do not lack the light of evening, we praise and glorify you through your Son Jesus Christ our Lord, through whom be glory and power and honour to you with the holy Spirit, both now and always and to the ages of ages. Amen.

> And all shall say:
> Amen.

> They shall rise, then, after supper and pray; and the boys and the virgins shall say psalms (ch. 25).

The continuation of this ruling is unclear. There is a mention of a Communion in a "mixed cup of the offering" and of taking "from the bishop's hand a little bit of bread," along with appropriate psalmody. Then come prescriptions concerning the common meal, with the bishop's participation, and the supper for widows. One reads also of the bishop giving instructions during meals:

> The faithful, as soon as they have woken and got up, before they turn to their work, shall pray to God, and so hasten to their work. If there is any verbal instruction, [they] should give

preference to this, and go to hear the word of God, to the comfort of [their] soul (ch. 41: reckoning in [their] heart that it is God whom [they] hear in the instructor). Let [them] hasten to the church where the Spirit flourishes (ch. 35).

The remaining rules propose a schedule of daily prayer patterned on the chronology of the passion of Christ: the prayers of the third and sixth hours refer to the crucifixion and the death of the Lord. The whole section ends with advice concerning prayer in the home and in the family.

These ancient testimonies too often give us only allusions so that it is impossible to know exactly what other assemblies were regularly convened in every church. We would love to know more about the practice of these common meals, or love feasts, but Ignatius' *Letter to the Smyrnaeans* contains only this admonition, without further particulars, "Without the bishop's supervision, no baptisms or love feasts are permitted" (8:2). This does not inform us any more than the Letter of Jude (v. 12) which mentions the love feasts only to denounce the excesses marring them.

### The Liturgy of Baptism

Several writers of the second and third centuries allude to baptism, such as Tertullian, whose testimony has been quoted above and who wrote a brief treatise on the subject but without much of a description of the ceremonial. Similarly, Justin wrote before him:

> Those who are persuaded and believe that the things we teach and say are true, and promise that they can live accordingly, are instructed to pray and beseech God with fasting for the remission of their past sins, while we pray and fast along with them. Then they are brought by us where there is water, and are reborn by the same manner of rebirth by which we ourselves were reborn; for they are then washed in the water in the name of God the Father and Master of all, and of our Saviour Jesus Christ, and of the Holy Spirit. . . . This washing is called illumination, since those who learn these things are illumined within. The illuminand is also washed in the name of Jesus Christ, who was crucified under Pontius Pilate, and in the name of the Holy Spirit, who through the prophets foretold everything about Jesus. . . .

> We, however, after thus washing the one who has been
> convinced and signified . . . assent, lead [that one] to those
> who are called [brothers and sisters], where they are assembled
> (*First Apology* 61; 65).

It is the *Apostolic Tradition* that gives us the best information on baptism. In chapters 15 to 21, it collected the elements of several baptismal rituals; however, we do not know in what communities they were in use. Nevertheless, the clues found in the *Apostolic Tradition* are in accord with the scattered allusions gleaned from other documents of the same period. Therefore, this document will be our guide in the presentation of the celebration of baptism and its preparation. We offer a few excerpts.

**The Preparation for Baptism, or the Catechumenate.** Whereas the writings of apostolic times give little emphasis to the preparation for baptism, the documents of the second and third centuries attest to a well-organized catechumenate. The *Apostolic Tradition* assigns it a three-year duration in two stages, each being ushered in by an examination of the candidates. The first admission entails an in-depth inquiry:

> Those who come forward for the first time to hear the word
> shall first be brought to the teachers before all the people arrive,
> and shall be questioned about their reason for coming to the
> faith. And those who have brought them shall bear witness
> about them, whether they are capable of hearing the word.
> They shall be questioned about their state of life: has he a wife?
> Is he the slave of a believer? . . . (ch. 15).

The inquiry is conducted by the teachers in charge of catechesis. The candidates are presented by trustworthy persons who must vouch for them. One recognizes in these texts the earliest mention of godparents at baptism. The inquiry bears on the reasons for the person's conversion, on the person's civil status and especially profession, hence a long list of trades and activities incompatible with the Christian faith. Those excluded are all persons involved in any activities connected with pagan cults or contrary to Christian morals, even civil servants and soldiers because they are required to take an oath of loyalty to the emperor, as well as school teachers and actors because they teach or enact pagan myths.

No information is provided about the content of the teaching given during the three years of preparation. In the community, the catechumens form a group by themselves, apart from the faithful. They do not receive the kiss of peace. On the other hand, after the catechetical meetings, the teacher prays and lays his hands over the catechumens.

The second phase of the catechumenate is the immediate preparation for baptism. But there is no indication of its duration. It opens with a new inquiry:

> And when those who are to receive baptism are chosen, let their life be examined: have they lived good lives when they were catechumens? Have they honoured the widows? Have they visited the sick? Have they done every kind of good work? And when those who brought them bear witness to each: '[He/She] has,' let them hear the gospel (ch. 20).

Then the candidates are exorcised daily by the laying on of hands. These exorcisms were not meant to drive out demons; rather they were purification rituals through which God was asked to free the candidates from the influence of pagan cults, regarded as demoniacal.

**The Celebration of Baptism.** As Justin has already demonstrated, the celebration of baptism took place on Sunday, the day of the communal assembly. According to Tertullian, "the Passover provides the most solemn day for baptism" (*Homily on Baptism* 19). But the *Apostolic Tradition* does not establish an explicit connection between baptism and the feast of Easter.

> Those who are to be baptized should be instructed to bathe and wash themselves on the Thursday. And if a woman is in her period, let her be put aside, and receive baptism another day. Those who are to receive baptism shall fast on the Friday. On the Saturday those who are to receive baptism shall be gathered in one place at the bishop's decision. They shall all be told to pray and kneel. And he shall lay his hand on them and exorcize all alien spirits, that they may flee out of them and never return into them. And when he has finished exorcizing them, he shall

> breathe on their faces; and when he has signed their foreheads,
> ears, and noses, he shall raise them up.
>     And they shall spend the whole night in vigil; they shall
> be read to and instructed. Those who are to be baptized shall
> not bring with them any other thing, except what each brings
> for the eucharist. For it is suitable that he who has been made
> worthy should offer an offering then (ch. 20).

The baptismal celebration takes place at dawn, at the end
of a watch, or Sunday vigil. According to ancient beliefs, night
is a long pregnancy of light, which Christians interpret, in a
paschal and baptismal symbolism, as a resurrection.

> At the time when the cock crows, first let prayer be made over
> the water. Let the water be flowing in the font or poured over
> it. Let it be thus unless there is some necessity; if the necessity
> is permanent and urgent, use what water you can find (ch. 20).

The text of this prayer over the water is unknown to us.
Preference is given to the water of a fountain (or a spring) or
to the water that flows from above ("poured over it"). Do we
have here an allusion to the channeling of water to Roman
cities by aqueducts? Nothing is said about the setting. Was
baptism celebrated outside, near a stream, or in the atrium of
a private residence, or in a place set aside for baptisms? In any
case, it was not celebrated in the assembly, for the newly baptized would be led there only after the baptismal immersion,
as we shall see later. This would be comparable to the house-
church of Dura-Europos, in which the room for baptisms—set
apart from the hall for assemblies—was identified by the presence of a basin and by iconographic decoration.

At the moment of baptismal immersion, the candidates
take off their clothes. The ritual determines the order in which
people receive baptism: first children, then men, then women.
It specifies that parents may answer in place of their children
if these are not yet able to answer personally. Two different oils
are prepared: the oil called oil of thanksgiving, over which the
bishop gives thanks and with which he will anoint the baptized, and the oil of exorcism.

For the renunciation of Satan, the *Apostolic Tradition* has
these instructions:

And when the priest takes each one of those who are to receive
baptism, he shall bid [each one] renounce, saying:

> I renounce you, Satan, and all your service and all your
> works.

And when each one has renounced all this, he shall anoint
[each one] with the oil of exorcism, saying to [each one]:

> Let every spirit depart from you.

And in this way he shall hand [each one] over naked to the
bishop or the priest who stands by the water to baptize (ch. 25).

In the words of renunciation, the term "service" (or
"pomp") designates the processions of pagan sacrifices and
the whole of idolatrous practices. The formula that accompa-
nies the anointing gives meaning to the rite: "Let every spirit
depart from you." The fact that several ministers are mentioned shows that this part of the baptismal ritual comes from
an important community where the number of candidates for
baptism demanded that in order to assure a smooth unfolding
of rites, the bishop be assisted by several attendants.

The threefold baptismal immersion is accompanied by the
confession of faith in the interrogative form:

> In the same way a deacon shall descend with [each person] into
> the water and say: . . .
>
> > [Do you believe in one God, the Father almighty ?] . . .
>
> And [the one] who receives shall say according to all this:
>
> > I believe in this way.
>
> And the giver, having his hand placed on [the person's] head,
> shall baptize [the person] once. And then he shall say:
>
> > Do you believe in Christ Jesus, the Son of God, who was
> > born from the Holy Spirit from the Virgin Mary, and was
> > crucified under Pontius Pilate, and died, and rose again
> > on the third day alive from the dead, and ascended into
> > heaven, and sits at the right hand of the Father, and will
> > come to judge the living and the dead?
>
> And when [the person] has said, 'I believe', [the person] shall
> be baptized again. And he shall say again:
>
> > Do you believe in the holy Spirit and the holy Church and
> > the resurrection of the flesh?

Then [the one] who is baptized shall say, 'I believe', and thus shall be baptized a third time (ch. 21).

After the triple immersion, the following rituals are mentioned in chapter 21:

1. An anointing by a presbyter with this formula, "I anoint you with holy oil in the name of Jesus Christ." This oil is no doubt the oil of thanksgiving prepared in the beginning of the celebration.
2. The putting on of clothes and the entrance into the church.
3. The laying on of hands by the bishop, together with an invocation.
4. An anointing done by the bishop with the oil of thanksgiving, accompanied by the formula, "I anoint you with holy oil in the name of God the Father almighty and Christ Jesus and the Holy Spirit."
5. The making of the sign of the cross by the bishop on the forehead of the newly baptized.
6. The kiss of peace given by the bishop to every newly baptized person with the salutation, "The Lord be with you." And the response, "And with your spirit."

This ensemble of rites appears too complex to have belonged to one single ritual, the more so as numbers 1 and 4 seem to be doublets. Other documents of the same period attest to a simpler ritual after the immersion. Thus Tertullian, who in his homily on baptism speaks of only one anointing and one laying on of hands.

There is another difficulty: the invocation mentioned in number 3 demands some explanation because it has come down to us under two different forms. In the Latin version of the *Apostolic Tradition*, which is the oldest, the words between square brackets are omitted; these are found only in the Coptic version.

Lord God, you have made them worthy to receive remission of sins through the laver of regeneration of the holy Spirit [make them worthy to be filled with the holy Spirit]: send upon them your grace, that they may serve you according to your will; for to you is glory, to Father and Son with the holy Spirit in the holy Church, both now and to the ages of ages. Amen (ch. 21).

The difference is an important one; for in the Latin version, baptism is acknowledged as "the laver of regeneration of the holy Spirit" and there is no connection between the laying on of hands and the Holy Spirit. In the other version, on the contrary, the gift of the Holy Spirit is linked to the laying on of hands by the bishop after baptism. The difference between the two versions reflects the variety of liturgical usages in those centuries: certain churches, especially in Syria, knew neither anointing nor laying on of hands after the baptismal immersion, and they linked the gift of the Holy Spirit to baptism itself. We find an echo of this in the *Didascalia* where it compares the reconciliation of sinners to baptism: "Indeed, the laying on of the hand shall be to [the person] instead of baptism—indeed, whether by the laying on of the hand, or by baptism, they receive the fellowship of the Holy Spirit" (10,114).

**The Baptismal Eucharist.** Baptism introduces new Christians to the Eucharist and the *Apostolic Tradition* supplies us with a few details of the rites peculiar to the baptismal Eucharist.

> [The newly baptized] shall pray together with all the people; they do not pray with the faithful until they have carried out all these things. And when they have prayed, they shall give the kiss of peace.

> And then the offering shall be presented by the deacons to the bishop; and he shall give thanks over the bread for the representation, which the Greeks call 'antitype,' of the body of Christ; and over the cup mixed with wine for the antitype, which the Greeks call 'likeness' of the blood which was shed for all who have believed in him; and over milk and honey mixed together in fulfillment of the promise which was made to the [ancestors], in which [God] said, 'a land flowing with milk and honey,' in which also Christ gave his flesh, through which those who believe are nourished like little children, making the bitterness of the heart sweet by the gentleness of his word; and over water, as an offering to signify the washing, that the inner [human being] also, which is the soul, may receive the same things as the body. . . .

And when he breaks the bread, in distributing fragments to each, he shall say;

The bread of heaven in Christ Jesus.

And [the one] who receives shall say;

Amen.

And if there are not enough presbyters, the deacons also shall hold the cups, and stand in good order and reverence: first, he who holds the water; second, the milk; third, the wine. And they who receive shall taste of each thrice, he who gives it saying:

In God the Father almighty.

And [the one] who receives shall say:

Amen.

And in the Lord Jesus Christ.

(Amen).

And in the Holy Spirit and the holy Church.

And [the person] shall say:

Amen.

So shall it be done with each one . . . (ch. 21).

The sharing in milk and honey is also attested by Tertullian in the excerpt quoted at the beginning of this chapter.

**Evolution of the Ritual of Baptism.** Whereas Justin was still very reticent concerning the ritual of baptism, the *Apostolic Tradition* bears witness to an institution more fully organized. It speaks of a lengthy preparation, with teaching and exorcisms, a ritual comprising several actions, that is, renunciation of Satan, anointing before and after baptism, a threefold immersion, a dialogue for the profession of faith, and post-baptismal rites. This development of the institution of baptism was due to the expansion of Christianity into a pagan environment. As they received candidates imbued with the idolatrous cults that pervaded their thinking and behavior, the Christian communities intensified the preparation for baptism in order to insure the seriousness of conversions, instruct minds in the knowledge of Scripture, and wean converts from their former idolatrous habits.

Since only immersion and the laying on of hands are of apostolic origin, people have wondered where the anointings integrated into the baptismal ritual come from. We probably have here the effect of the customs of antiquity, where baths were ordinarily followed by massages with oil. If this is so, the baptismal anointings would have to be seen as the Christianization of cultural customs (inculturation). Christians transformed these commonplace customs into expressive gestures visually showing the effects of the baptismal mystery.

According to tradition, well attested in these ancient documents and set in relief in the present ritual of the baptism of adults, the liturgy of baptism unites into one celebration baptismal immersion, the conferring of the gifts of the Holy Spirit, and the Eucharist.

### Ministries and Ordinations

Christian communities attribute to certain of their members a particular status, either because of the ministries they are engaged in, their manner of life, or their participation in the offerings—these conditions being found singly or together in various persons. The *Apostolic Tradition* establishes the following list (chs. 2–14): bishop, presbyter, deacon, confessor, widow, reader, virgin, subdeacon, healer. The document proves that a ritual of ordination had been instituted to ask for and manifest the Holy Spirit's coming down upon those who are charged with ministries. It specifies in which cases the laying on of hands is foreseen, that is, for the first three ministries on the list, and it supplies the elements of the ritual as well as the formulary for these three ordinations.

For the episcopal ordination, this church order prescribes the following ritual:

> Let him be ordained bishop who has been chosen by all the people; and when he has been named and accepted by all, let the people assemble, together with the presbytery and those bishops who are present, on the Lord's day. When all give consent, they shall lay hands on him, and the presbytery shall stand by and be still. And all shall keep silence, praying in their hearts for the descent of the Spirit; after which one of the bishops present, being asked by all, shall lay his hand on him who is being ordained bishop, and pray, saying . . . (ch. 2).

The prayer of ordination given by this document has been integrated into the present Roman ritual. It contains an anamnesis (recalling) of God's initiatives in the organization of God's people, an epiclesis (calling down) of the Holy Spirit on the person being ordained, and a petition that he worthily fulfill the episcopal ministry.

The same pattern is present in the rituals for the ordination of presbyters and deacons (chs. 7–8). In both, we find a brief mention of the rite of the laying on of hands by the bishop and of the presence of clergy and then the prayer of ordination. This comprises an epiclesis in both ordinations. The Holy Spirit is qualified depending upon the ministry for which it is invoked: guiding Spirit, according to Psalm 51:14, for bishops; Spirit of grace and counsel for presbyters, Spirit of grace and zeal for deacons. For readers (ch. 11), the ruling of the *Apostolic Tradition* prescribes only the handing over of the book, without the laying on of hands. For subdeacons (ch. 13), we read only that they are designated by that name. Confessors of the faith are admitted to the diaconate and the presbyterate without the laying on of hands, but it is required for their admission to the episcopate (ch. 9). This special treatment can be explained thus: like martyrs, confessors have been ordered to renounce their faith and have submitted to torture, but not unto death. Their confession of faith and their victory over torture prove that they are filled with the Holy Spirit; therefore, the laying on of hands is not appropriate.

For admission to the order of widows and for virgins and healers, the laying on of hands is excluded (chs. 10, 12, 14). The church order adduces reasons for each of these three situations: the order of widows is not a ministry; the choice of virginity is a matter of personal decision; and for healers, the facts themselves will demonstrate whether they have this gift or not.

The three ministries of bishop, presbyter, and deacon are well attested in the documentation of this time. On the other hand, as far as the other ministries are concerned, there are differences between churches. In Rome, an already quoted list going back to 251, the time of Pope Cornelius, enumerates subdeacons, acolytes, exorcists, readers, and doorkeepers. At the same time in Carthage, Cyprian mentions the same ministries except that of doorkeeper.

When speaking of the functions exercised in communities, the documentation of the period rarely distinguishes between the liturgical and non-liturgical. The goal of all ministries is the pastoral service of the community; and the synaxes are not only cultic, as were the sacrifices in the Jerusalem Temple, but are intended to regulate all the actions of the community. The prayers of ordination in the *Apostolic Tradition* recognize both the priestly dimension and pastoral function of ministries, and the *Didascalia* stresses the teaching duties incumbent on bishops.

Justin had already spoken of the deacons' service: they participate in the distribution of Communion in the assembly and then carry their share to the absent. In the other documents, which are a little more explicit, the deacons' ministry is described as a service to the community, to its members, and above all to the bishop. (See the *Apostolic Tradition*, chs. 8 and 34). Further, the *Didascalia* prescribes the assistance of deaconesses for the baptismal anointing of women and for the service of sick or destitute Christian women (16,156-158).

As to the recruitment of the ministers for the community, these ancient church orders focus primarily on qualities that the candidates should possess in a way similar to that of the New Testament pastoral letters. In another vein, Cyprian left us a piece of information on the way people were called to ministries when persecution decimated the community: "The small number of the people who remain here being barely able to assume the daily tasks, there was a need to ordain and send some new ones" (Letter 29). For this recruitment, Cyprian consults the clergy, presbyters in particular, but also the community at large.

### The Reconciliation of Penitents

During apostolic times, remission of sins usually meant baptism. How to deal with sins committed after baptism was a subject rarely broached. Solutions could be radical, as in the cases of Ananias and Sapphira and the Corinthian man guilty of incest. For the latter, Paul seems to have ordered exclusion, whereas the former two were struck dead (Acts 5:1-10; 1 Cor

5:5). At that time, Christian communities still doubted the possibility of readmitting sinners into the community.

But by the third century, it was generally recognized that the Church had the power to remit sins by penance, considered a second baptism. However, the rigorist current denied the possibility of pardon for certain sins regarded as very grievous—such as adultery and debauchery—in order not to encourage vice and to safeguard the dignity of Christian living, especially in the eyes of catechumens. But persecutions soon led the communities to create a genuine institution to deal with repentant sinners.

Indeed, the severe persecution of Decius (249–251) caused numerous apostasies: ordered by the Roman power to deny their faith by sacrificing to the idols, a certain number of Christians yielded for fear of torture and death. Some of these apostates repented afterwards. New pastoral questions arose in the communities: How should one deal with these repentant persons, especially when finding themselves in danger of death because of an epidemic—as happened in Carthage—they implored the community to grant them pardon? Answers were not unanimous and these differences of opinion in their turn provoked grave conflicts between rigorists, in particular Novatian in Rome, and partisans of mercy, such as Pope Cornelius and Bishop Cyprian.

Putting into practice the Lord's advice (Matt 10:23), Cyprian had fled his city of Carthage. He remained in communication with his church, and the letters he exchanged with his clergy show us that there existed a pastoral penitential system for the reconciliation of the lapsi, "those who had fallen" in the course of the persecution. They were placed into three distinct categories, according to the gravity of their apostasy.

- the *libellatici* were those who, without having formally apostatized, had requested or accepted fraudulent certificates testifying that they had sacrificed and therefore had denied their faith. At the least, they were a cause of scandal in the community.

- the *thurificati* were those who had thrown a few grains of incense on the gods' altar. This gesture was the equivalent of a formal apostasy.

• the *sacrificati* were those who had completely apostatized since they now participated in all the ceremonies of the pagan cult, from the sacrifice of victims to the sacrificial meal.

During the persecution, Cyprian settled the case of those apostates who were sick and in danger of death: the repentant sinner who had been sponsored by a martyr or a confessor of the faith could confess his or her sin to a presbyter or a deacon and be reconciled by the laying on of hands.

After the persecution, Cyprian convened a council of the local bishops in order to fix the penitential discipline. It was decided that the *libellatici* could be immediately reconciled, but the *thurificati* and *sacrificati* were submitted to a long penance. However, no sin, even the most grievous, was excluded from ecclesial reconciliation, contrary to the rigorists' opinion. It was the bishop's responsibility to direct the penitential course of action and the community's to verify the conversion of the penitents. These persons were set apart from the community in the same way as the catechumens: admitted to the assemblies for the readings and teaching, they were excluded from the prayer of the faithful and the eucharistic oblation. Reconciliation was signaled by the laying on of hands by the bishop and the other clergy, but it was acknowledged by all that only God gives pardon.

In the midst of persecution, the repentant apostates turned to martyrs and confessors of the faith, asking them to intercede in their favor in order to obtain an immediate reconciliation; the martyrs' and confessors' sufferings were credited with the power of compensating the sin of the lapsi—a compensation ascertained by notes of recommendation *(libelli)*. Cyprian treats of this practice in his letters in order to regulate it and prevent abuses.

Only grave sins were subject to the penitential institution. As for what were called "everyday sins," Cyprian said they could be forgiven by the recitation of the Our Father, good works, and almsgiving.

Some documents from the same period show that other churches had established for all grave sins penitential institutions

similar to that of Carthage. The *Didascalia*, for instance, indicates that the catechumenate was the model followed for the
organization of reconciliation rites:

> "As a heathen," thus, "and as a publican" let [that one] be ac-
> counted by you who has been convicted of evil deed and of
> falsehood. And afterwards, if [the person] repent as in the case
> when the heathen desire and promise to repent, and say "we
> believe," we receive them into the congregation that they may
> hear the word. But we do not communicate with them until
> they receive the seal and become perfected. Thus also do we
> not communicate with these until they show the fruits of re-
> pentance. . . .
>
> But you shall by no means hinder them to enter the church
> and to hear the word, O bishop. For even our Lord and Savior
> did not completely put away and cast out publicans and sin-
> ners, but did even eat with them. . . . And so as you baptize a
> heathen and receive [that one], so also lay the hand upon [this
> one] while everyone is praying . . . and then bring [the person]
> in and let [the person] communicate with the church (10,113-
> 114).

## Liturgies for the Martyrs and the Dead

For burial and the cult of the dead, common traditions had
developed throughout numerous provinces of the Roman
Empire: at the funeral, family and friends of the deceased
gathered at the grave side and shared a funerary meal, at
which the dead person was supposed to be present. The same
ritual was observed every year on the anniversary of burial.
Christians kept these customs while modifying them in order
to express their faith in the resurrection, especially in the case
of a martyr.

It is in the *Martyrdom of Polycarp* that we find the oldest
evocation of a meeting planned for a martyr's anniversary.
This is in a letter from the church of Smyrna, whose bishop
Polycarp had been; the letter was written less than one year
after the facts. The date of the martyrdom is not established
with certainty, perhaps February 23, 166. After Polycarp's suffering and death, Christians had wanted to claim his body, but
the magistrates sought to prevent them from doing so:

[They were] ignorant that we can never forsake Christ, who suffered for the salvation of the whole world . . . nor can we ever worship any other. For we worship this One as Son of God, but we love the martyrs as disciples and imitators of the Lord, deservedly so, because of their unsurpassable devotion to their own King and Teacher. . . . [The centurion] burned [the body]. So we later took up his bones, more precious than costly stones and more valuable than gold, and laid them away in a suitable place. There the Lord will permit us, so far as possible, to gather together in joy and gladness to celebrate the day of his martyrdom as a birthday, in memory of those athletes who have gone before, and to train and make ready those who are to come hereafter.[7]

In order to remember the celebration of anniversaries, communities prepared lists of their martyrs, with mention of the date of martyrdom and the location of the grave.

In the *Didascalia*, we find a mention of assemblies in honor of other deceased persons. It is in the course of a discussion concerning the rules of ritual purity observed by the Jews and forbidding contact with corpses.

You . . . shall be assembled even in the cemeteries, and read the holy Scriptures, and without observance [of ritual purity] complete your services and your intercessions to God and offer an acceptable eucharist, the likeness of the body of the kingdom of Christ, in your congregations and in your cemeteries and on the departures of them that sleep among you—pure bread that is prepared in fire and sanctified through an invocation—and without doubting pray and offer for those who are asleep. . . .

On this account then do you approach without restraint to those who rest, and you shall not declare (them) unclean . . . (26,243-244).

### The Paschal Feast

In the second and third centuries, Christian time derived its rhythm from the recurrence of Sunday, which is the day of the Lord and the weekly celebration of the resurrection. The only yearly feast mentioned is that of Easter. Most churches celebrated it on the Sunday following the first full moon of spring. But according to a tradition established in Asia Minor and supposed to have originated with John the Apostle, a few communities celebrated it on the 14th of Nisan (the fourteenth day of the first moon of spring) whatever the day of the week. These differences in date gave rise to grave conflicts, especially with Pope Victor (ca. 195).

For the liturgical aspect, the *Didascalia* is the most informative document. It describes the traditions in force in some Syrian churches. These traditions reflect the concern of these communities to distance themselves from Judaism by carefully avoiding the celebration of their feasts on the same days as the Jews; for instance, they fasted at the time of the Jewish Passover because of the Lord's death and in memory of his word, "The days will come when the bridegroom is taken away from them, and then they will fast on that day" (Mark 2:20).

As a consequence, this tradition divides the narrative of the passion into six sections, from Monday to Saturday, in order to extend the fast over the whole of the Great Week. On Monday, the plot against Jesus is recalled and the Last Supper is advanced to Tuesday evening. The appearances before Caiaphas and Pilate are assigned to the following days. Since the communities which the *Didascalia* addresses had daily meetings, morning and evening, all year around, it is likely that this chronology of the passion determined the selection of readings on every day of the Great Week.

> You shall fast in the days of the Pascha from the tenth, which is the second day of the week . . . until the third hour in the night after the Sabbath (21,198-199).
>
> Therefore it is required of you, [brothers and sisters], in the days of the Pascha, to follow closely with (all) diligence and to perform your fast with all care. And begin when your [brothers and sisters] who are of the people perform the Passover. For when our Lord and teacher ate the Passover with us, He was delivered up by Judas after that hour, and immediately we began to be grieved because He was taken from us (21,196).
>
> Wherever, then, the fourteenth of the Pascha may fall, observe it in this way. Indeed, neither the month nor the day corresponds in time every year, but it is changed. When therefore that people performs the Passover, do you fast. And be careful to complete your vigil within their (feast of) unleavened bread. However, on the first day of the week be glad at all times; in-

deed, [one] is guilty of sin, [who] torments [one's] soul on the first of the week (21,202).

For the night of Saturday to Sunday, the *Didascalia* describes how the paschal vigil was celebrated:

> You shall assemble together and watch and keep vigil all night with prayers and intercessions, and with the reading of the prophets, and with the Gospel and with the psalms with fear and trembling and with assiduous supplication . . . (21,198-199).
>
> And then offer your oblations. And after this eat and enjoy yourselves, and rejoice and be glad, because the earnest of our resurrection, Christ, is risen . . . (21,199-200).
>
> On the resurrection of Christ, rejoice and be glad for their [the Jewish people] sake, and break your fast.
>
> And the gains of your fast of six days offer to the Lord God. However, let those of you whose worldly possession is abounding serve those who are poor and needy and refresh them diligently that the reward of your fast may be received (21,201).

We find another clue concerning Easter in chapter 33 of the *Apostolic Tradition*, where it makes allusion to the fifty days following Easter in order to prohibit fasting during this time. But the text says no more than this.

### The Oil of the Sick

In chapter 5, after the Eucharistic Prayer, the *Apostolic Tradition* offers a formulary for the blessing of the oil and mentions its therapeutic effects:

> If anyone offers oil, (the bishop) shall render thanks in the same way as for the offering of bread and wine, not saying it word for word, but to similar effect, saying:
>
>> O God, sanctifier of this oil, as you give health to those who are anointed and receive that with which you anointed kings, priests, and prophets, so may it give strength to all those who taste it, and health to all that are anointed with it.

This formulary alludes to the uses this sanctified oil will have: the sick ingest it or anoint themselves with it. Such practices were common in the Mediterranean countries where the olive tree is cultivated, because olive oil, known for its therapeutic virtues, is one of the basic products used in daily life. For the anointing of the sick, this document does not prescribe that ministers of the community be present.

## Marriage

The early church orders do not treat of marriage. The reason for this is that among Christians as well as among Jews and in conformity with the usages of antiquity, marriage was an essentially familial rite. It was the father of the family who united the couple in the home. The presence of the community minister was not deemed necessary. However, to guarantee ecclesial recognition and adhesion to the Christian ideal, Ignatius asked that the bishop be consulted for marriages (*Letter to Polycarp* 5.2), and Tertullian, in an allusion difficult to interpret, intimates that marriage is sanctified by participation in the Sunday Eucharist of the community.

## Conclusion

A rapid comparison with the present state of the liturgy allows us to realize that in the second and third centuries, almost all liturgical institutions were well established, although of course under forms that were still elementary. Christian communities came together regularly for the Sunday Eucharist and daily for morning and evening meetings. The organization of ministries had progressed since apostolic times in order to insure liturgical, pastoral, and charitable services for larger communities. For entry into certain ministries, the liturgy of ordination took shape, stressing the call of the candidates and the manifestation of the Holy Spirit in them. As to entrance into the community through baptism and the reconciliation of repentant sinners, more complex institutions were set up in order to guarantee the serious character of conversions to Jesus Christ and to protect the holiness of communities.

On the whole, the forms of the liturgy at that time appear still simple and spare. Christian communities had definitively broken away from Judaism and rejected observances judged incompatible with the gospel. But being the Church of Jesus Christ, they considered themselves the only legitimate heirs of the Old Covenant and the sole legitimate Israel. The turning of these communities toward pagan masses favored this distancing from Jewish observances, but at the same time, the adoption of other cultic practices added to the rites inherited from apostolic times: baptismal anointings, funeral rites.

However, the numerous conversions among pagans led to the development of Christian teaching, which was at the time conceivable only as based entirely on the Holy Scriptures. For communities in a precarious situation, whether clandestine or tolerated, regular assemblies were the principal place where catechumens and faithful were instructed. Whereas the liturgical ceremonial was simple and spare, the biblical readings and all manner of preaching must have been very amply developed. This state of affairs would continue through the following period, to the point that Christian faith came to completely permeate civic institutions and pagan culture came to be forgotten.

Chapter 4

# The Liturgy in the Roman Empire after the Peace of the Church

In 313, by what is called the Edict of Milan, Emperors Licinius and Constantine put an end to the persecutions against Christians and ordered the restitution of their places of worship. Christian communities were now to enjoy a definitely more favorable status in the Roman Empire, and in 380, Emperor Theodosius recognized Christianity as the state religion. All of this resulted in massive conversions and in the expansion of the communities. It became necessary to adapt the institutions of the churches to these new conditions.

The founding of new communities and the ease of communication insured by the imperial administration led the churches to improve their territorial organization. The bishops of more important cities were given primacy, and even jurisdiction, over their colleagues of the same district. Thus, the Council of Nicaea (325) legitimated the rights of the bishops of Rome, Alexandria, and Antioch and the honors due to Jerusalem. Later on, the Councils of Constantinople (381) and Chalcedon (451) recognized the primacy of honor—after Rome—of Constantinople, the new capital of the Empire. Around these five cities, Rome, Constantinople, Alexandria, Antioch, and Jerusalem, the five great patriarchates were established. But the bishops of other important metropolises— such as Carthage, Caesarea of Cappadocia, the capitals of independent kingdoms, and so on—also exercised jurisdiction over neighboring cities.

This organization into districts had repercussions in the liturgical domain because the churches of the same province tended to take their inspiration from the traditions of the metropolitan church. The regular convening of local synods also contributed to a certain unity in rituals, although without abolishing the autonomy of the local churches. However, every church felt obliged—and in the fourth century, this concern was very prevalent—to seek a connection with apostolic foundations, albeit through the intermediary of other persons named in the New Testament. Two examples: Caesarea of Palestine claimed to have had Zaccheus as its first bishop; the church of Berea in Macedonia believed it had been founded by Onesimus, the freed slave Paul mentions in his letter to Philemon.

The division of the Roman Empire into two parts, West and East, was definitive from 364 on, under Valentinian and Valens. However, shortly afterwards, because of the barbarian invasions and the fall of Rome and of its last emperor, whatever remained of the Western Empire officially became a province of the Eastern Empire, while in fact being delivered into the invaders' power. In the course of the sixth century, the Byzantines recaptured a great part of Italy and the city of Rome from the invaders and established Greek colonies there. Emperor Justinian (537–565) restored the unity of the Empire for some time. Communication and exchanges between Latins and Greeks continued during the better part of the first millennium, and the flourishing of Byzantium in the cultural domain profoundly marked the West. An evident proof of this is the iconography of the Carolingian and Romanesque periods, which show the strong influence of Byzantine traditions.

Four of the great patriarchates were located in the Eastern part of the Empire: Constantinople, Alexandria, Antioch, and Jerusalem. Their common language was Greek. Rome was the only patriarchate of the Western Empire and its language was Latin. In its capacity of new Rome, Constantinople progressively gained primacy among the Eastern patriarchates. This position was strengthened as a result of the schism of the churches of Egypt and Syria after the Council of Chalcedon (451). The patriarchates of Antioch, Alexandria, and Jerusalem broke away from Constantinople, which remained the sole guarantor of orthodoxy in the East. Later on, the traditions of the church of Constantinople were imposed on all other churches that had remained under imperial jurisdiction, even on those which Byzantium reconstituted in the territories that had embraced the schism, Syria and Egypt. At the same time, the churches separated from Constantinople and Greek culture developed their own traditions in the local tongues (Coptic, Syriac, Armenian).

The de facto separation between the Eastern and Western Churches was rendered definitive only by the deplorable excommunication of the Patriarch of Constantinople by the legate of Pope Leo IX in 1054. (This excommunication was revoked in 1965). Until the middle of the eleventh century, the relationship between the churches of Rome and Constantinople had endured in spite of the vicissitudes of history. The church of Constantinople, then flourishing, acknowledged with less than eagerness the apostolic authority of the church of Rome. From ancient capital, Rome had shrunk to the size of a small town because of war with the Goths (536–555). In addition, in 554, the imperial administration established the seat of the prefecture of Italy in Ravenna, not Rome.

After the era of persecution, the churches knew periods of expansion, of reorganization, of reform; nevertheless, they rarely lived in genuine peace. From the fourth century on, they had to contend with the conceptual heritage of Greek culture, local autonomous tendencies, personal rivalries; these confrontations generated an unending series of schisms and heresies. Besides, the West was ravaged by successive barbarian invasions which decimated populations, eliminated their structures—political, cultural, and religious—almost completely annihilating the effects of the first evangelization.

Christian communities very painfully felt this ruin and perceived the sack of Rome by Alaric in 410 as an outrage. Pagans blamed Christians, reproaching them for having banished the gods, protectors of the city. It was in this context that Augustine wrote *The City of God*.

For its part, the East was progressively amputated by the Moslem conquest less than one century after the apogee of Justinian's reign. Then came the grave crisis of iconoclasm (730–870). To the east and south of what remained of the

Empire, in Egypt, Syria-Palestine, Mesopotamia, and beyond, the churches that had separated themselves from Constantinople (after 451) found themselves gradually encircled by Islam and reduced to the state of minorities, which contributed to rigidly fixing their traditions.

### The Sources

The liturgical institutions of the fourth and fifth centuries are well known, thanks to abundant documentation comprising writings of different genres: church orders, homilies, catecheses, letters, stories. These documents complement one another and allow us to reconstruct almost entirely the rituals in use for several churches.

**A Compilation of Earlier Church Orders.** Among church orders, the most important bears a title which may appear anachronistic to us: *Apostolic Constitutions.* What we have here is a compilation in which three documents, already met in the preceding chapter, were collected and reworked: the *Didascalia, Didache,* and *Apostolic Tradition.* Several other documents were added, in particular a series of blessings of synagogal origin and rituals. The whole thing is presented as a collection of traditions coming from the apostles and assembled by Clement of Rome, Peter's companion. This appeal to apostolic origin was supposed to guarantee the authority of the document; nothing prevents us from believing that certain traditions collected here were of apostolic origin, but the bulk of the work is made up of developments of what had germinated in the first Christian communities and of adaptations to new circumstances.

This assemblage of rulings deals with pastoral and canonical questions, but more particularly with liturgical celebrations. It seems to have been put together in Syria, in the region of Antioch, about 380. It has come down to us in its original version, Greek. The institutions it describes were those of a large community.

**Catechesis and Preaching.** The fourth and fifth centuries are called "the golden age of patristics" because of the abundance and quality of the works Christian authors wrote during that period; among them were numerous bishops who received the title of "Fathers (*Patres* in Latin) of the Church." In this literature are many sermons and catecheses that allude to certain aspects of the liturgy. The systematic study of these allusions has allowed us to reconstruct a large part of the rituals practiced in several churches: Hippo with Augustine, Antioch and Constantinople with John Chrysostom, Caesarea of Cappadocia with Basil, and so on.

As far as catecheses are concerned, it was in Jerusalem that the most available document originated, the *Protocatechesis and the Five Mystagogical Catecheses* of Cyril of Jerusalem.[1] After a preliminary catechesis, the bishop of Jerusalem commented on the creed in twenty-four baptismal catecheses during Lent for the instruction of the catechumens who were going to receive baptism at Easter.

The following five catecheses, called mystagogical, are especially replete with information for the study of liturgy: during paschal week, the preacher unveiled for the newly baptized the mysteries of baptism, the signing with chrism (which became the Confirmation in the West), and the Eucharist. This preaching was particularly important in the fourth century because of the numerous adult baptisms. Mystagogical catecheses authored by other preachers have also come down to us: those of John Chrysostom, Theodore of Mopsuestia, Ambrose of Milan.

It is through the channel of such a catechesis of Ambrose that the oldest excerpt from the Eucharistic Prayer called the "Roman Canon" has reached us (the present Eucharistic Prayer number 1).

> You have learned, therefore, that what you receive is the body of Christ. Will you know that it is consecrated by heavenly words? Hear what the words are. The priest speaks. "Make for us", he says, "this oblation approved, ratified, reasonable, acceptable, seeing that it is the figure of the body and blood of our Lord Jesus Christ, who the day before he suffered *took bread* in his holy hands, and *looked up to heaven* to you, holy Father, almighty, everlasting God. . ." (*On the Sacraments* 4.20-21).[2]

**Letters.** In the correspondence of several bishops of the fourth and fifth centuries, we can find allusions to celebrations.

Some letters treat of ecclesiastical or liturgical traditions, in particular the letters of the bishops of Rome and other metropolises. Two of Pope Innocent I, one addressed to Bishop Exuperius of Toulouse in 405 and the other to Decentius of Gubbio in 416, are of great interest. They treat of several liturgical questions: the reconciliation of penitents, the place of the kiss of peace, confirmation, the anointing of the sick, and so on.[3]

**Euchologia.** These are manuals containing Eucharistic Prayers, ordination prayers, the blessing of water, instructions given by deacons, and so on. The term has remained in use in Byzantine churches and designates the book of formularies used today in the liturgy. The oldest euchologic collections have been transmitted to us in church orders that preserved them, in particular, the *Apostolic Tradition* and *Apostolic Constitutions*.

But a euchologion of the fourth century has been discovered; coming from Egypt and written on a single sheet, it bears the name of Serapion and is usually referred to as the *Euchologion of Serapion*.[4] However, because of theological divergences, we cannot attribute it to Bishop Serapion of Thmuis in Lower Egypt (d. after 362), who was a friend of Athanasius. The collection contains thirty prayers destined to be used at the Eucharist, baptism, ordinations, the anointing of the sick, and the liturgy for the dead. We do not know how in fact this euchologion was utilized, for what purpose it was composed, because the text of the prayers appears without any indication concerning their use.

**A Treatise.** A Greek theologian from the end of the fifth century, inspired by Neoplatonism, wrote several treatises which had a very large readership both in the East and the West, especially in mystical circles. He is known under the pseudonym of Dionysius the Areopagite. One of his treatises gives commentaries on the liturgical celebrations of his time, probably as they were performed in Antioch. The title of this treatise is the *Ecclesiastical Hierarchy*.[5]

**A Travel Journal.** Egeria, a pious woman from northern Spain or southern France, brought back from her travels in the East, about the years 381-384, a very detailed description of the celebrations in which she had participated in Jerusalem: daily liturgy, weekly cycle, and yearly feasts.[6]

## The Assemblies

The new policy of the Empire towards Christians put an end to the relative clandestinity of their assemblies. Henceforth, these could be organized in total freedom and even move into public space. Besides, powerful people in the imperial administration officially attended Christian celebrations, transferring the religious aspects of their offices to the new state religion.

As a consequence of the mass conversions encouraged by these new circumstances, communities grew, their liturgical assemblies gained in amplitude and necessitated an appropriate organization. Hence, the multiplication of ministries and more meticulous regulation concerning the synaxes in order to insure good order and dignity. Owing to the spirit of the time, very respectful of hierarchies, there were a number of distinct groups in the assembly, each with its assigned place. A passage in the *Apostolic Constitutions* concerning the order in which to receive Communion enumerates the different groups present in the assemblies:

> And after this, the bishop shall partake, then the presbyters, deacons, sub-deacons, the readers, the singers, and the ascetics; and [then] among the women, the deaconesses, the virgins and the widows; then the children; and then all the people in order with reverence and godly fear, [and] without uproar (8.13.15).[7]

In another section of the same document, two comparisons are invoked to justify the assignment of places in the assembly: that of ships with their crews and passengers and that of the sheepfold in which "the shepherds place all the creatures distinctly, I mean goats and sheep, according to their kind and age, and still every one runs together, like to its like" (2.57). Since this excerpt is a new rendering of a similar passage in the *Didascalia* quoted above, we can appreciate the evolution from one period to another.

In the course of the fourth and fifth centuries, due to many conversions, the communities received an important contingent of adult candidates for baptism. These people seem to have been tolerated in or admitted to the assemblies even before their inscription into the catechumenate. Then, they were called "hearers." They were asked to leave when the moment for prayer came:

> All standing up, the deacon shall ascend the bema [high place], and proclaim: [Let] none of the hearers [remain]! [Let] none of the unbelievers [remain]. And silence being established, he shall say: Catechumens, pray! (*Apostolic Constitutions* 8.6.2-3).

Once admitted to the preparation for baptism, candidates remained catechumens for several years, often beyond the three-year minimum. For this reason, the catechumens formed an important group in the assemblies. They were ranged with penitents and victims of demoniac possession. These three groups received the benefit of the prayers offered by the assembly, but they could not participate in the prayer of the baptized, not only during the Eucharist but even in the services of daily praise:

> When it is evening, O bishop, you shall assemble the Church; and after the recitation of the psalm at the lighting of the lamps, the deacon shall bid prayers for the catechumens, for the energumens [possessed], for those about to be illuminated, and for the penitents. . . . After they have been dismissed, the deacon shall say: "All we, the faithful, let us pray to the Lord" (*Apostolic Constitutions* 8.35.2; 8.36.1).

Because of this influx of converts, a very important portion of the assemblies was devoted to teaching. Egeria mentions this for Jerusalem, and her account agrees with the practice of other churches:

> But you should note that here it is usual for any presbyter who has taken his seat to preach, if he so wishes, and when they have finished there is a sermon by the bishop. The object of having this preaching every Sunday is to make sure that the people will continually be learning about the Bible and the love of God.
>
> Because of all the preaching it is a long time before the dismissal, which takes place not before ten or eleven o'clock.

> [On] the Fortieth Day after Epiphany . . . all the pres-
> byters preach first, then the bishop, and they interpret the pas-
> sage from the Gospel about Joseph and Mary taking the Lord
> to the Temple. . . (25.1-2; 26).

In these Jerusalem assemblies as described by Egeria, we
discern three groups. First, the Christians of the local community, together with their catechumens. Then, the monks and
nuns established in Jerusalem. Finally, the pilgrims staying for
a while in the city. Each one participates—according to his or
her possibilities—in the same celebrations in the great basilica (Martyrium) and in the rotunda of the Church of the
Resurrection (the Anastasis).

> All the doors of the Anastasis are opened before cock-crow
> each day and the *"monazontes* and *parthenae,"* as they call them
> here, come in, and also some lay men and women, at least those
> who are willing to wake at such an early hour. . . .
> As soon as dawn comes, they start the Morning Hymns,
> and the bishop with his clergy comes and joins them. . . . He
> blesses the catechumens, and then [says] another prayer and
> blesses the faithful (24.1-2).

The adoption of the Christian religion by the Empire
brought about the gradual Christianization of society, institutions, and culture. The clergy obtained a privileged status;
schools gradually exchanged mythologies for the Bible;
monachism developed. With the spread of infant baptism and
the reading and teaching of sacred Scripture in the home and
schools, the teaching function of liturgical assemblies diminished. Consequently, the time allotted to the readings and
teaching was shortened. At the same time, there was an increased consciousness of the grandeur of the mysteries being
celebrated and an amplification of the sensible and aesthetic
aspects of worship in imitation of the heavenly liturgy:
singing, ceremonial, setting, and decoration were given great
importance. The ceremonial of the imperial court, especially in
Byzantium, offered models of glorious displays.

This evolution of the liturgy toward more solemn forms
owes much to the influence of Pseudo-Dionysius who, in his
commentaries, focused on the contemplation of heavenly reali-

ties. Whereas the documents of the previous era treated of liturgical realities mainly under the communal aspect since they were addressed principally to pastors, the purpose of Pseudo-Dionysius had a more personal orientation. This last trait is characteristic of the periods of Christendom: when the whole population is Christian, the pastoral effort aims less at constituting communities than at fostering the spiritual progress of individuals. Here is an excerpt from the commentaries of Pseudo-Dionysius; it concerns the eucharistic liturgy:

> When these sacred hymns, with their summaries of holy truths, have prepared our spirits to be at one with what we shall shortly celebrate, when they have attuned us to the divine harmony and have brought us into accord not only with divine realities but with our individual selves and with others in such a way that we make up one homogeneous choir of sacred [persons], then whatever resumé and whatever opaque outline is offered by the sacred chanting of the psalmody is expanded by the more numerous, more understandable images and proclamations in the sacred readings of the holy texts (*Ecclesiastical Hierarchy* 3.3.5).

However, in a Christianity of the masses, it was necessary to constantly urge the faithful to attend the celebrations. The fact is that like the crowds mentioned in the Gospels, those of the following centuries were first of all worried about the difficulties of daily life, especially in times of invasions, wars, epidemics, and other calamities. They expected religion to provide them healing, health, and protection from threats and dangers. This expectation created conditions favorable to the extension of the cult of martyrs and other saints, first at their places of burial, then through the veneration of relics and images (icons). Such veneration took place either during yearly celebrations or on the occasion of pilgrimages; through these contacts, believers sought to share in a power victorious over evil. As a result, in many cases, the faithful preferred devotional practices over liturgical assemblies.

## The Basilicas

After 313, Christian communities, now freed from clandestinity and blessed with a robust growth, needed more spacious places of worship. At that time, the cities of the Empire had at their disposal a certain type of building responding to such needs, the basilica. It was a large hall with a nave whose space could be enlarged by the addition of lateral naves communicating through colonnades with this central nave. The roof rested on wooden rafters or more rarely on vaults. Christian communities adopted this type of building, to which they added a transept and apse. In spite of baroque facings and reconstructions, some great Roman basilicas give us an idea of the architecture and dimensions of these edifices: St. John Lateran, St. Mary Major, St. Paul, St. Sabina, and so on. The imperial administration contributed to the building of Christian basilicas as it had previously done for the cults of the city. Emperor Constantine and his mother, Helena, promoted a vast building program, certain realizations of which—the basilicas called "Constantinian"—still exist in Rome, Jerusalem, Bethlehem, and elsewhere. The basilica model inspired the construction of innumerable churches in all regions of the Empire and in the West until the Middle Ages.

However, in the East under the reign of Emperor Justinian (527–565), architects began to have recourse to the cupola, which allowed the enlargement of the central space. The model of this genre is the Church of Santa Sophia in Constantinople (present-day Istanbul). An earlier basilica erected by Constantine having been destroyed during an insurrection in 532, Emperor Justinian had a larger edifice built, and on a new plan. It was inaugurated on December 27, 537. Its distinctive feature was that the central cupola, having a diameter of thirty-four yards, was built above a gallery of windows. Thus, the light came down from the heights. This phenomenon was interpreted in a symbolic and mystical way according to the doctrine of Pseudo-Dionysius, as is shown by Procopius:

> Upon this circle rests the huge spherical dome which makes the structure exceptionally beautiful. Yet it seems not to rest upon solid masonry, but to cover the space with its golden dome suspended from Heaven. . . . The whole ceiling is overlaid with pure gold, which adds glory to the beauty, yet the light reflected from the stones prevails, shining out in rivalry with the gold. . . .

> And whenever anyone enters this church to pray, [that person] understands at once that it is not by any human power or skill, but by the influence of God, that this work has been so finely turned (*Buildings* 1.1).[8]

Afterwards, all Byzantine buildings were modelled on Santa Sophia and the liturgy itself adapted to this architecture.

In ancient civilizations, the placement of houses, but even more, that of cultic edifices, in relation to the sun, source of light, has always been the object of special attention. In Christianity, a widespread tradition dictated that the building be oriented, that is, have the apse to the east. There exist written attestations to this tradition, like the excerpt from the *Didascalia* quoted above (see p. 39) and the repetition of this same ruling, with additions, in the *Apostolic Constitutions*:

> And first, let the building be oblong, turned towards the east, with the *pastophoria* on each side at the east end, [and] so it will be like a ship. . . (2.57.1).
>
> After this, let all rise up with one consent, and looking towards the east . . . pray to God, who ascended up to the heaven of heavens towards the east, remembering also that humankind's first home, paradise, was in the east, whence the first humans . . . were expelled (2.57.14).

The eschatological meaning of the orientation rests upon an extrapolation of Psalm 68(67):34 (in the Greek version): it is in the east that Christ ascended to heaven and from there that he will come back. Basil the Great expressed a similar thought:

> We all pray facing the East . . . . We are seeking Paradise, our old [homeland], which God planted in the East in Eden (Gen 2:8). We all stand for prayer on Sunday . . . . We stand for prayer on the day of the Resurrection to remind ourselves of the graces we have been given: not only because we have been raised with Christ and are obliged to seek the things that are above (Col 3:1), but also because Sunday seems to be an image of the age to come (*On the Holy Spirit*, 27.66).

Archeological research has shown that this tradition was generally kept in all the regions of the Empire, but also that it was not absolute. Thus, in Rome, the earliest basilicas are turned in different directions; and several, among them St.

John Lateran and St. Peter at the Vatican, have the apse clearly facing the west.

The interior arrangement of the basilicas comprised some sort of lectern for the readings, seats for the ministers, the altar, and railings in order to define the reserved spaces. The arrangement of these different elements varied according to regions. Thus, in old Syrian churches, archaeologists have discovered a platform *(bema)*, with throne, bench, and lecterns, placed in the middle of the nave. This plan was akin to that of Jewish synagogues. In contrast, it has been shown that the altar stood in the middle of the nave of a church in North Africa. But, progressively, in all churches, the ministers' seats, the lecterns for the readings, and the altar were all placed in front of the apse or in the apse.

In Rome, in the basilicas built in cemeteries in honor of martyrs, the altar was placed above the holy tomb, and an architectural feature, called the *confessio*, allowed access to the tomb. This *confessio* was a semi-circular excavation with stairs. This feature was maintained even through the successive modifications the edifices underwent, as one can see, for instance, in St. Peter in the Vatican. Moreover, it was even introduced in the basilicas that were not built over holy tombs, as is the case for St. John Lateran and St. Mary Major. One replaced the absent holy tomb by relics. Early churches were dedicated to the mysteries of the faith; some traces still remain: the basilica of the Lateran first bore the name of the Savior and that of Constantinople was dedicated to divine Wisdom *(Sophia)*. But in many cases, the name given to a church is that of the martyr whose tomb it shelters or whose relics it preserves.

According to iconographic documents and vestiges found in the ruins of ancient churches, curtains were fixed on porticoes at the entrance of the sanctuary in order to conceal or reveal the altar at certain moments of the liturgy, a practice still observed in Eastern liturgies. The main function of the removal of the veil is to signify the manifestation of God's glory in the liturgy as the actualization of the incarnation.

Following the architectural traditions of the Roman Empire, Constantinian basilicas were richly decorated. Later on, these decorations became a mode of expression: through the medium of mosaics or frescoes covering the apse, the image becomes the complement of words. Indeed, as can be seen in ancient basilicas, in particular in Rome and Ravenna, and in the rare edifices which in the East were not destroyed by iconoclasts, an iconographic tradition came gradually to dominate and its programs were followed even in the Romanesque art of the West and, to our own day, in the East.

This iconography visually suggests the mystery of the liturgy, that is, the communion of the assembly with the invisible God made visible by the one who is God's image, Christ. We have here august scenes comprising the representation—figurative or symbolic—of Christ in glory, in the center, surmounted by the Father's hand and the dove of the Holy Spirit and surrounded by apostles and saints in the presence of the heavenly court (angels). The cosmic dimension is suggested by a conventional representation of the universe with its different elements, sky, earth, sea, rivers, animals. This iconography renders visible to the assembly its participation in the heavenly liturgy; it reminds believers that through the Eucharist, the Church enters the sanctuary of heaven and that the whole universe enters it as well.

After the victory of Orthodoxy over iconoclasm (870), we find in Byzantine churches that besides mural paintings, the entrance of the apse was covered with icons to such an extent that it became a partition, called the iconostasis. This tradition developed especially in Russia. The iconographic programs of Byzantine churches were fixed with great precision, appointing places to representations of persons and scenes according to strict hierarchies. This agreed with the meaning which liturgical commentators assigned to the different parts of the church: the vault represents heaven; the doors of the iconostasis symbolize either Christ, inasmuch as he has access to the Father, or Mary, as the entrance of God into our humanity; the curtains are symbols of the revelation of holy mysteries; and so on.

## The Eucharistic Celebration

Justin's testimony quoted above (see pp. 39–40) demonstrates that the main features of the eucharistic celebration

were fixed as early as the second century. In the course of the
following centuries, we notice the development of certain
parts of the celebration and especially the evolution of the
Eucharistic Prayer. In addition, there is an increase in the number of commentaries explaining the rituals.

**The Ceremonial of the Eucharistic Liturgy.** We find in the
*Apostolic Constitutions* an overall presentation of the eucharistic ceremonial. It is presented—anachronistically—as coming
from the apostles themselves, but the information concurs
with other Syrian testimonies of the fourth century.

> Let the reader, standing on a high place in the middle, read the
> books of Moses, of Joshua the son of Nun, of the Judges, and of
> the Kings and of the Chronicles, and those written after the re-
> turn from the captivity; and besides these, the books of Job and
> of Solomon, and of the sixteen prophets. After two lessons have
> been read, let some other person sing the hymns of David, and
> let the people join in singing the refrains. Afterwards let our
> Acts be read, and the Epistles of Paul our fellow-worker, which
> he sent to the Churches under the directions of the Holy Spirit;
> and after that let a presbyter or a deacon read the Gospels,
> those which I, Matthew, and John have delivered to you, and
> those which the fellow-workers of Paul, Luke and Mark, com-
> piled and left to you. And while the Gospel is read, let all the
> presbyters and deacons, and the whole people, stand in pro-
> found silence. . . . Next let the presbyters, each in turn, not all
> together, exhort the people, and lastly the bishop, as captain of
> the ship.
>
> Let the doorkeepers stand at the men's entrances to ob-
> serve them, and the deaconesses at those of the women. . . .
> Let the deacon attend to the placings, so that everyone who
> comes in may go to his or her proper place, and not sit next to
> the entrance. In the same way let the deacon keep watch on the
> people, that nobody may whisper or sleep or laugh or nod or
> beckon. . . .
>
> After this, let all rise up with one consent and, looking to-
> wards the east, after the departure of the catechumens and the
> penitents, pray to God, who ascended up to the heaven of
> heavens, towards the east. . . . After the prayer, let some of the
> deacons concern themselves with the offering of the eucharist,
> ministering with fear to the body of the Lord, and let the others
> crowd and keep them silent. Let the deacon who is at the

bishop's side say to the people: 'Let no one have any quarrel with another! Let no one come in hypocrisy!' Then let the men salute the men, and the women the women, with the kiss of peace in the Lord, but let none do it deceitfully, like Judas who betrayed the Lord with a kiss.

After this, let the deacon pray for the whole Church, for the whole world, and for the several parts of it, and for abundance of the fruits of the earth, for the priests and rulers, for the bishop, for the king, and for universal peace. Then let the bishop, praying for peace upon the people, bless them. . . .

After this let the sacrifice take place, all the people standing and praying in silence: and when the oblation has been made, let every group by itself partake in order of the Lord's body and of the precious blood, and approach with reverence and godly fear, as to the body of a king. Let the women approach with their heads covered. . . . But let the doors be watched, lest any unbeliever, or any not yet initiated, come in (2.57.5-10,13-14,15-19,21).

Besides this description of the ritual, the *Apostolic Constitutions* have also collected, in book 8, the texts of diaconal directions and priestly prayers: prayers for the dismissal of the catechumens, the possessed, and the penitents; general intercessions; Eucharistic Prayer; and prayers after Communion (8.6-15). In the ceremonial of book 8, the kiss of peace comes after the general intercessions, whereas in the excerpt just quoted, the two are reversed; but this inversion seems fortuitous.

We do not have documents as detailed on the practice of other churches. However, by interpreting various allusions gleaned here and there, we can surmise that, overall, the eucharistic ritual was almost identical in all the churches in the fourth century, except for the place of the kiss of peace, which in Africa and Rome followed the Eucharistic Prayer.

In the excerpt quoted above, the eucharistic assembly is presided over by the bishop. It is surrounded and served by the different ministries. It gathers the whole of the local community, as was recommended in Ignatius' *Letter to the Smyrnaeans*: "Where the bishop is present, there let the congregation gather" (8:2). But with the growth of communities and the multiplication of churches, presbyters were more and more often called upon to preside at the Eucharist in places where the bishop could not be present. This must have been the case for a long time in large cities where it was impossible to convene the local community in a single place. The same letter of Ignatius already mentioned that a delegate of the bishop presided at the Eucharist: "You should regard that Eucharist as valid which is celebrated either by the bishop or by someone he authorizes" (8:1).

The *Apostolic Constitutions* above lists the following elements: readings, psalmody, preaching, kiss of peace, general intercessions and their concluding prayer, bringing of the gifts, Eucharistic Prayer, and Communion. There is no mention of an entrance ritual. From allusions made by John Chrysostom and Augustine—and they agree—we know that the opening of the celebration was then very short: the bishop entered the church, went to his place, and saluted the assembly ("The Lord (or Peace) be with you!").

The readings began immediately. The ritual of the *Apostolic Constitutions* indicates the books to be read, without specifying the number of readings. These were chosen from the whole Bible and offered in the following order: Old Testament, epistles, gospel. Other sources specify three, five, or seven readings, even twelve during vigils. As for preaching, what is said about the contribution of several presbyters and the bishop corresponds to Egeria's testimony quoted above (see pp. 71–72).

We know of two forms of general intercessions. First, a series of diaconal biddings (up to sixteen or eighteen) with repeated responses by the assembly (*Kyrie eleison*) and concluding prayer, as in the *Apostolic Constitutions* and the Byzantine liturgy. Second, diaconal biddings followed by silent prayer on the part of the assembly and by a prayer said by the priest; this form was in use in Rome and North Africa, and a witness to it remains in the present Roman liturgy on Good Friday.

According to most witnesses of that period, only the deacons seem to have had the duty of bringing the gifts: they brought to the altar the bread and wine selected from the offerings received before the celebration. Theodore of Mopsuestia offered a mystagogical commentary on this function:

We must see Christ who now goes and is led to his passion; at another moment, again he is lying for us on the altar in order to be immolated. This is why those deacons who lay the altar cloths on the altar offer us the image of the linens used at the burial. . . . And the bishop begins to give [the kiss of] peace; the church herald [that is, the deacon] orders the people to give peace one to another. . . . Then the bishop washes his hands. . . . The lists of names of the living and the dead written on church tablets are read. . . . [then comes the Eucharistic Prayer] *(Catechetical Homily 15)*.[9]

The tablets mentioned here were used to write the names of persons to be recommended to God during the oblation. Other contemporary documents also allude to them. The letter of Pope Innocent I to Decentius so attests to the Roman practice, represented by the memorial of the living which has remained in place at the beginning of the present Eucharistic Prayer 1.

Book 8 of the *Apostolic Constitutions* has preserved a very extensive Eucharistic Prayer (8.12.4-51). We do not know how widely it was diffused. Nevertheless, its structure corresponds to that of the Eucharistic Prayers of the Eastern churches; it has inspired our own Eucharistic Prayer 4. It is a unified composition depicting a vast synthesis of the economy of salvation in order to proclaim its effective realization in the Eucharist.

Other Eucharistic Prayers (or anaphoras) received their definitive form in the same period. It has been established that Basil the Great (d. 379) modified and enlarged an already existing formulary. He gave his name to this Eucharistic Prayer, still in use in Byzantine churches on certain occasions, among them the Sundays in Lent. Called the Anaphora of St. Basil, it has the following general outline:[10]

> • Initial dialogue (the first salutation corresponds to 2 Cor 13:13).
> • Initial formula of blessing: "God, almighty Father, how fitting and proper it is to the majesty of your holiness to praise you, to sing to you, to bless you, to glorify you. . . ."
> • Contemplation of God's mystery: "Father of our Lord Jesus Christ . . . who is the image of your goodness

. . . through whom the Holy Spirit has been manifested.
. . ."

• Participation in the heavenly liturgy and singing of the biblical Trisagion ("Holy, holy, holy, Lord of Hosts. . . .")

• Anamnesis of God's wondrous deeds and of the economy of salvation, from creation to the incarnation.

• Narrative of the eucharistic institution.

• Prayer of the eucharistic oblation: Christological anamnesis and offering of the oblation.

• Epiclesis: "We implore you . . . to send your Holy Spirit on us and these gifts . . . let it bless them and sanctify them. . . ."

• Prayers of intercession, within the communion of saints.

• Final doxology.

Like Basil, John Chrysostom adapted an existing formulary, and his name has remained attached to it. This Eucharistic Prayer, called the Liturgy of St. John Chrysostom, is the one most often used in Byzantine churches.

The Eucharistic Prayer (or Canon) of the Roman church differs from those of the Eastern churches in that it contains changing parts, especially prefaces. The preface is a thanksgiving which changes with the liturgical times and feasts that are celebrated, whereas the Eastern Eucharistic Prayers always give thanks for the whole of the mystery of salvation. Before the imposition of uniformity in the ninth century, other Western churches had their own eucharistic formulas. And even afterwards, some kept traces of these formulas, among them the Milanese (Ambrosian) and Iberian (Mozarabic) liturgies.

In several commentaries of the fourth century, the rites of Communion immediately follow the Eucharistic Prayer. As a consequence, the place of the Our Father in the ancient liturgies is difficult to determine. The *Apostolic Constitutions* are silent on this subject. On the other hand, Cyril of Jerusalem comments on the Lord's Prayer in his catechesis on the eucharistic celebration.

The assemblies having become large, the material preparation for Communion by the breaking of the bread took time.

Rituals and commentaries mention the formulas of acclamation and the psalms that accompanied the distribution of the bread and wine made Eucharist. For their part, the catechists explained the way one should receive Communion, as did Cyril of Jerusalem:

> Make your left hand like a throne for your right, which is about to receive the King. And having cupped your palm, receive the Body of Christ, saying, "Amen." Then after you have with care hallowed your eyes by touching them with the Holy Body, partake thereof; taking heed lest you lose any of it. . . .
>
> Approach also the Cup of His Blood. Not stretching forth your hands, but bending and saying with worship and reverence, "Amen," be hallowed by partaking also of the blood of Christ. And while the moisture is still upon your lips, touching it with your hands, hallow your eyes and brow and other senses. Then wait for the prayer and give thanks to God, who has accounted you worthy of such great mysteries (*Mystagogical Catecheses* 5.21-22).

The prayer mentioned at the end of this passage was that of the postcommunion. Several documents have preserved for us examples of this prayer, for instance the *Euchologion* of Sarapion:

> We give thanks to you, Master, for you have called the erring and taken notice of those who have sinned, and you set aside the threat against us. You yielded to your love of humanity and you wiped it away in repentance, and rejected it according to your own knowledge. We give you thanks because you have given us communion of the body and blood. Bless us, bless this people, make us to have a portion with the body and the blood. Through your only-begotten son through whom the glory and the power are yours in [the] holy Spirit both now and forever and to all the ages of ages (no. 4).

**Roman Traditions.** Although the eucharistic rituals agree on the whole from one church to the other, certain communities stood out by their own pastoral practices. Thus, we know two Roman traditions expressing the communion between eucharistic assemblies. We speak first of the rite of the *fermentum* (leaven) attested to in several passages. The most explicit is found in a letter of Pope Innocent I in 416:

As to the *fermentum* which we send on Sundays to the diverse "titles," it is superfluous for you to consult us because here all the churches are within the walls of the city. On Sunday, their presbyters are not able to join us because of the people entrusted to their care; the *fermentum* [from our Eucharist] is therefore sent to them by acolytes so that they will not consider themselves separated from communion with us, especially on that day. But I do not think that this practice should be adopted in the rural regions of the diocese because the sacrament should not be carried any great distance. For our part, we do not send the *fermentum* to the priests appointed to the churches established in cemeteries (*Letter to Decentius*, pp. 27–29).

The pope distinguishes two kinds of churches: those inside the walls of Rome, called "titles," and those outside the walls of the city, in the cemeteries (churches in honor of martyrs and built over their tombs) and in the country. The priests who celebrate with their people on Sunday in the "titles" receive fragments of the bread made Eucharist at the pope's Mass. This was done as a sign of communion: it was the *fermentum*. The pope deemed there was absolutely no reason to adopt this custom in a little town like Gubbio.

The other tradition in force in Rome to manifest the communion between communities concerned the stational Mass celebrated in the pope's absence. On the great solemnities (Christmas, Epiphany, Easter, Pentecost) and during Lent and Paschal Time, the church of Rome, clergy and people, joined the pope in one of the great basilicas or in one of the neighborhood churches ("titles"). It was the "station." When the pope was unable to be present, communion with him was shown by a significative rite: the priest replacing the pope placed in the cup a fragment of the bread that had been made Eucharist by the pope during one of the great solemnities and kept for this purpose: this was the *immixtio*.

**Roman Traditions and Byzantine Traditions.** From the fifth century on, the Roman and Byzantine liturgies evolved along different lines. Among the traits that distinguish the two, one can note—and this has already been mentioned with regard to the Eucharistic Prayer—the organization of the liturgical prayer (as distinguished from the readings). In the Byzantine liturgy, the greater number of the prayers of the eucharistic celebration remain the same, whereas in the Roman liturgy, many pieces (songs and prayers) change with each celebration. When we evaluate these differences, we must remember that in the Latin churches, the Mass has become a daily event, while in the Eastern churches, it is primarily dominical.

Concerning the church of Rome, we have a few testimonies on the earliest manifestations of this variability of Mass prayers. We think in particular of the Mass formulary which Pope Gelasius had ordered composed in 495 on the occasion of a serious pastoral difficulty: Christians had wished to reestablish the Lupercalia. Fecundity rites at their origin, these festivities were celebrated on the fifteenth of February and featured a race of naked men, brandishing thongs with which they struck the women crowding in their way. These practices degenerated into excesses and debauchery. Pope Gelasius had forbidden Christians to take part in the Lupercalia, but some people had ignored the prohibition. In the course of successive liturgical celebrations, the conflict was evoked in the liturgical prayer: the prayers and prefaces of eighteen Sundays contain warnings, then intercessions for the sinners, entreaties for those who repented, and finally thanksgiving for the reconciliation, according to the successive phases of the conflict (see Sources chrétiennes 65). Elements of these Mass formularies, composed in particular circumstances, found their place in the annual cycle later on when the first collections, distant ancestors of the *Roman Missal*, were constituted.

In the Byzantine liturgy, except for the readings and sung pieces, the components of the eucharistic formulary do not vary with each celebration, except that there is a choice between two Eucharistic Prayers, *Divine Liturgy of Saint John Chrysostom* and *Divine Liturgy of Saint Basil*. The Byzantine Euchologion adds to these two the *Liturgy of the Presanctified*, which is a liturgy of Communion, therefore without a Eucharistic Prayer, available on the weekdays in Lent. The prayers of Byzantine liturgies are more developed than those in the formularies of Roman Masses.

The two practices have a different impact on the participation of the assembly and the personal memory of the faithful. A formulary that is repeated every Sunday is soon known by heart and nurtures the faith, whereas a short prayer heard but once is remembered only if the formulation helps memorization. The effects of both regimens must be taken into consideration in a pastoral study: How are the liturgical prayers received by the faithful?

The ambiance of the celebration is even more strikingly different between the Roman and Byzantine liturgies. This fact was already noted in the tenth century in a chronicle from the reign of Vladimir I, Grand Prince of Kiev. The chronicle records the impressions of a delegation of boyars who had gone to gain knowledge of the different religions of their neighbors, including the Romano-Germanic Empire and Byzantium.

> Afterwards, we went to the Germans and we saw many offices performed in their churches, but we saw nothing of beauty. We went to the Greeks, who took us to the place where they render worship to God. And we did not know whether we were in heaven or on earth. For there is neither a comparable wonder, nor such a beauty on earth, and we are unable to express either. But we do know that it is there that God dwells with humankind.[11]

However, both Rome and Byzantium solemnized the eucharistic liturgy. In Rome, according to the descriptions of the *Ordines Romani* (ceremonial directions), there existed a meticulous etiquette in the way the pope was surrounded; in the movements of the many ministers, officials, and clergy; and in the organization of processions. In Byzantium, in addition to the influence of the imperial ceremonial, the development of the ritual was inspired by the representation of the events of the salvific incarnation, as we saw above in the commentaries of Theodore of Mopsuestia concerning the way the gifts were brought to the altar (see p. 81). The movements of the eucharistic celebration were (and are) set in relation to the actions of Christ at his first coming: the Little Entrance (with the carrying of the gospel book) represents Jesus' itinerant preaching; the Great Entrance represents his entrance into the passion; the different parts of the eucharistic Prayer are referred to the moments of passion, resurrection, and Pentecost.

No doubt, there were some distortions in the application of this intuition, and the commentaries diverge in certain interpretations. Nevertheless, this understanding of the eucharistic liturgy manifests the unity of salvation by concretely recognizing in the present celebration the events of the passion and resurrection. The Byzantine tradition has remained faithful to this line of interpretation, and one of the masterpieces in this domain was written at the end of the fourteenth century by Nicholas Cabasilas, *The Explanation of the Divine Liturgy.*

In the West, the Middle Ages also produced commentaries on the eucharistic liturgy, but they tended to lose their way in an excessive use of allegory. Besides, as the peoples' participation in the liturgy became more and more tenuous, these commentaries focused on an edifying and moralizing interpretation at the expense of the properly liturgical and mystagogical signification. As an example, in Amalarius of Metz (775–832), we find this commentary on the ceremonial of readings:

> Why [do we make the sign of the cross] precisely on the forehead? Because the forehead is the seat of shame. . . . We . . . believe that we are saved by the Crucified One. . . . We believe that this name protects us. This is why we make the sign of the cross on the forehead. . . . The two candles that are carried in front of the gospel book designate the Law and the Prophets, who have preceded the gospel teaching. The censer evokes all the virtues emanating from the life of Christ. . . . The place of the candles shows that the Law and the Prophets [came before] the gospel.[12]

Nicholas Cabasilas, a Byzantine, commented on other aspects of the ceremonial of readings:

> Why do we praise God before the readings from Holy Scripture? Because it is fitting to do so for all those things which [God] does not cease to bestow upon us, and especially for so great a benefit as listening to the Divine Word. For the Epistle in particular our praise is mingled with supplication. . . . For the Gospel our supplication consists simply in the hymn itself, that we may know that the Gospel represents Christ, and that [one] who has found Christ has obtained all that [one] could desire. For therein is the Bridegroom, and those who possess all things need ask for nothing more.[13]

Commentary is moral when it takes the rites as an occasion to formulate rules of behavior. It is liturgical when it explains the internal coherence of the rites. It is mystical when it fosters a personal relationship with God which is not only on the plane of knowledge. In his entire work, Nicholas Cabasilas urges his readers to live the liturgy as a "life in Christ," according to the title of another of his writings.

Why did the Eastern and Western churches diverge so widely in the practice and understanding of the liturgy? Some explanations drawn from the political and cultural spheres can be offered. It is a fact that from the sixth to the fifteenth centuries, the Byzantine church lived in a universe favorable to the development of its institutions, in spite of difficulties and crises. This made cultural progress possible, whose agents were spiritual persons and theologians, both clerical and lay. The missionary conquest within the Empire having been completed, efforts were no longer devoted to the conversion of pagans but to the strengthening of the heritage at the level of thought and institutions.

Now, it belongs to the very being and mode of behavior of the Byzantine churches to place the liturgy at the center of the life of communities, and theological reflection develops in relation to the liturgy. Conversely, theological debates have left their mark on the liturgy: the addition of professions of faith by formulas or acclamations, formation of new rites or reinterpretation of existing rites. Thus, the insertion of the hymn *O Monogenes* ("O Only Son") before the readings is attributed to an initiative of theological conciliation taken by Justinian about the year 532:

> Only-begotten Son and Word of God, you who are immortal, and who deigned to take a body from the Holy Mother of God and always Virgin Mary, and who, without change, became human, and were crucified, O Christ God, and through your death overpowered death. You are One of the Holy Trinity, glorified with the Father and the Holy Spirit. Save us.[14]

Here is another example of theology influencing liturgy, the rite of the *zeon*, attested to for the first time in the sixth century. Before Communion, the celebrant not only places a fragment of the consecrated bread in the cup—this is the *commix-tion*—but also adds a little hot water—this is the *zeon*. These rites proclaim the resurrection: the body and the blood of Christ are again united, and the addition of the *zeon* signifies the warming up of the blood and, therefore, the life that results from the resurrection. An accompanying formula has been added to the rite, "for the fullness of the Holy Spirit." In the same way the resurrection of the Lord was accomplished by the Holy Spirit, so the presence of the Risen One in the gifts made Eucharist is obtained by the invocation of the Holy Spirit. Thus, the evolution made in the understanding of the mystery of the Eucharist in its correspondences with the mystery of the incarnation has caused the addition of new rites or new interpretations in the Byzantine liturgy.

While political and cultural circumstances allowed the Byzantine church to develop, not without difficulties of course, and stimulated the progress of liturgical institutions and theological reflection, the West was undergoing the upheaval of the barbarian invasions with all their political, social, and cultural consequences. The battered churches were hardly in a position conducive to theological reflection. The few centers that endured, such as Rome, Northern Italy, Provence, and Spain, succeeded only with difficulty in preserving the heritage. In the intervals of peace when restorations became possible, the first task was the mission within in order to convert and Christianize the masses still deeply steeped in paganism and far from being able to appreciate all the riches of the liturgical celebrations.

When the time came for theological restoration in the West, the Church had lost the proper equilibrium as far as the liturgy was concerned: this was regarded as the business of clerics, and private Masses were considered the norm. The medieval theology of the Eucharist took its point of departure from the private Mass. We shall come back to this point.

### The Synaxes on Weekdays

From the fourth century on, we have many texts concerning the daily praise celebrated in the churches. Practices varied, but in any case, there were gatherings of the local communities, therefore of the Christian people. On this subject, one of the most obvious testimonies comes to us from Eusebius of Caesarea, commenting on Psalm 64:9 (65:8):

> For it is surely no small sign of God's power that through the whole world in the churches of God at the morning rising of the sun and at the evening hours, hymns, praises, and truly divine delights are offered to God. God's delights are indeed the hymns sent up everywhere on earth in his Church at the times of morning and evening.[15]

This welling up of praise in the Christian communities corresponded to the vocation of the churches. Indeed, called, as was the first Israel, to glorify God in the name of all creation, the first Christian communities saw how cities rendered a public cult to demons while they themselves were forced to keep their celebrations clandestine. No doubt, they longed to worship the only true God in a worthy manner according to the patterns that apocalyptic visions attributed to the heavenly court. As a consequence, as soon as the freedom of cult was fully granted, the churches let the praise—up to now kept hushed—publicly resound.

As in the preceding period, evening and morning praise were the essential observances. But certain communities also gathered for nightly celebrations, for instance, in Caesarea of Cappadocia:

> In our community the people rise at night in order to go to the house of prayer; and in sorrow, in affliction, and in uninterrupted tears, we confess our faith in God. At last, we stand up after the prayers of supplication and we begin the psalmody. First, having divided ourselves into two groups, we send the chant back and forth from one group to the other. Thus, we make the texts our own in a deeper way and gain attentive and recollected hearts. Then, entrusting to one person the duty of intoning the chant, all the rest respond. After spending the night in a psalmody diversified in this way, with prayers interspersed between psalms, at daybreak, all together, with one mouth and one heart, send up to the Lord the psalm of confession, each one applying to himself or herself the words of repentance.[16]

Also in the same period, diverse forms of monastic life arose or developed. Among them, urban monachism took an important part in the celebration of daily praise to the point of assuming its direction, and even of replacing the local community.

The *Apostolic Constitutions* (8.35-39) describe how these daily liturgies were conducted in what one would call today a "base community," a local church presided over by the bishop. The offices of morning and evening followed the same plan:

- Evening or morning psalm (respectively, Psalms 140(141) and 62(63).
- Ceremonial of dismissal of the catechumens, the possessed, those about to be baptized, and the penitents, as was done in the course of the eucharistic liturgy.
- Prayer of the assembly according to the pattern of the general intercessions: announcements by the deacons and concluding prayer by the bishop.
- Blessing of the assembly: the deacon called the assembly to prostrate and the bishop recited the prayer over the people.
- Formula of dismissal.

This liturgy was simple and repetitious: the same psalms were repeated every day. It corresponded to the situation and possibilities of the local communities. It was pedagogical: since these services were destined for all the faithful, it was necessary to limit the choice of texts to what the assembly could memorize (there were no pocketbooks for the faithful in those days!). In contrast, monastic communities, whose ideal was to pray continually, integrated the whole psalter into the Liturgy of the Hours.

In Jerusalem, the daily offices were more developed, which can be explained by the presence of monks and nuns, as has been mentioned above (see p. 72). Egeria describes in great detail the daily offices there and notes what seemed to her a particularity:

What I found most impressive about all this was that the psalms and antiphons they use are always appropriate, whether at night, in the early morning, at the day prayers at midday or three o'clock, or at Lucernare [lighting of the lamps, the evening office]. Everything is suitable, appropriate, and relevant to what is being done (Egeria 25.5).

## The Baptismal Liturgy

Because of the numerous conversions to the Christian faith, the fourth and fifth centuries were the golden age of the catechumenate and baptismal liturgy. About the year 400, one estimates that in a single year, there were as many as one thousand candidates for baptism during the Easter vigil in large cities like Antioch and Constantinople. At that time, many Christians were baptized as adults. This was the case with people like Ambrose (who was at least 34), Jerome (who was at least 20), Paulinus (who was 37), Augustine (who was 33), John Chrysostom (who was about 20).

The overall ritual had already been fixed in the preceding period; the ceremonial was barely enriched, but it was organized in a more institutional way. For admission to the catechumenate, several documents mention rites of reception. Thus, Augustine narrates how his baptism was postponed:

Even as a boy, of course, I had heard of an eternal life. . . . And I was signed with the sign of His Cross and seasoned with His salt as I came new from the womb of my mother (*Confessions* 1.11).[17]

The sign of the cross and the giving of the salt were accompanied by a prayer with the laying on of hands. Augustine describes the organization of the catechesis in a little guide, *The First Catechetical Instruction*, he wrote for a deacon of Carthage who was in charge of welcoming the pagans and giving them their first initiation to the faith:

The narration is complete when the beginner is first instructed from the text: *In the beginning God created heaven and earth*, down to the present period of Church history. That does not mean, however, that we ought to repeat verbatim the whole [of the Scriptures including the Acts of the Apostles]. . . . But we ought to present all the matter in a general and comprehensive summary, choosing certain of the more remarkable facts that are heard with greater pleasure and constitute the cardinal points in history (*First Instruction* 3.5).[18]

For the benefit of his addressee, Augustine supplies two models of catechesis, adapted to different publics. Both are an elementary presentation of the economy of salvation on the basis of biblical traditions.

**Lent, Preparation for Baptism.** Many catechumens delayed the decisive step; this was the case with Augustine himself. In view of this, preachers made pressing appeals before Lent in order to urge those people who had long been catechumens to ask for baptism; this was conferred principally during the Easter vigil (Pentecost and, in the East, Epiphany were also baptismal days, according to local traditions). The preparation was spread over several weeks in such a way as to accommodate the forty days of fast, which are the origin of Lent. Depending on whether Saturday was a fast day (West) or not (East), the number of weeks varied, as Egeria remarked when comparing the Jerusalem usages with those of her native country:

> In our part of the world we observe forty days before Easter, but here they keep eight weeks. It makes eight weeks because there is no fasting on the Sundays or the Saturdays (except one of them, which is a fast because it is Easter vigil). . . . So the eight weeks, less eight Sundays and seven Saturdays . . . make forty-one fast days. The local name for Lent is *Heortae*.
>
> I feel I should add something about the way they instruct those who are to be baptized at Easter. Names must be given in before the first day of Lent, which means that a presbyter takes down all the names before the start of the eight weeks for which Lent lasts here, as I have told you. . . . On the second day of Lent . . . one by one those seeking baptism are brought up, men coming with their [godfathers] and women with their [godmothers]. As they come in one by one, the bishop asks their neighbours about them: "Is this person leading a good life? Does [she] respect [her] parents? Is he a drunkard or a boaster?" . . . And if his inquiries show him that someone has not committed any of these misdeeds, he himself puts down [the person's] name; but if someone is guilty [that one] is told to go away. . . .
>
> Those who are preparing for baptism during the season of the Lenten fast go to be exorcized by the clergy first thing in the morning. . . . As soon as that has taken place, the bishop's

chair is placed in the Great Church, the Martyrium, and all those to be baptized, the men and the women, sit round him in a circle. There is a place where the [godfathers] and [godmothers] stand, and any of the people who want to listen (the faithful, of course) can come and sit down (Egeria 27.1; 45; 46.1).

This class of catechumens was thus designated *electi, competentes,* or *illuminandi,* that is, "elect," "candidates," or "illuminands." Lent was an intensive preparation for these people, but the whole community was associated with them. At the daily assemblies, the illuminands were exorcised and instructed. Egeria gives us the following program for this catechesis (ch. 46):

1. Explanation of sacred Scripture: the bishop "first relat[es] the literal meaning of each passage, then interpret[s] its spiritual meaning."

2. Exposition of the resurrection and the faith.

3. Exposition of the baptismal Creed (the *Credo*) article by article: this was what in Rome was called *Traditio Symboli.*

On Palm Sunday, the catechumens recited the Creed that had been explained to them; it was the *Redditio Symboli.*

In North Africa and Rome, these sessions were called "scrutinies." They allowed for the verification of whether the devil still dominated the candidates, which could be judged by their behavior. Through rites of exsufflation (breathing out or blowing), one provoked the devil and ordered it to depart. In Rome, the scrutinies took place on the third, fourth, and fifth Sundays of Lent. The readings as well as the formularies of these three Sunday liturgies were dominated by the catechumenate: gospels of the Samaritan woman, the man born blind, and the resurrection of Lazarus, preceded by readings from the Old Testament dealing with the waters of Meribah (Num 20:1-13), purification by water (Isa 1:16-17), and a resurrection (1 Kgs 17:17-24).

**The Celebration of Baptism.** The basilicas had a place appropriate for baptizing, the baptistry. Many ruins of baptistries remain in North Africa, Provence, Turkey, Palestine, and other places. But several baptistries have been preserved, more or less in their original state: the Lateran, Aix-en-Provence, Fréjus,

Poitiers. The edifice comprised a central room with the baptismal font and sometimes annexes, probably for the anointings. At the paschal vigil, while the community prayed, listened to readings, and sang psalms, the candidates went to the baptistry, then rejoined the community for the Eucharist.

In the fourth century, the ceremonial for the renunciation of Satan and the allegiance to Christ was lengthened. Cyril of Jerusalem compared it to the crossing of the Red Sea and described it as follows (*Mystagogical Catecheses* 1.2,4,9):

- The candidates enter the vestibule of the baptistry.
- Standing, they turn to the west, "the region of sensible darkness" (the place whence comes night at sunset); they are commanded to extend their hands.
- They pronounce the formula of renunciation: "I renounce you, Satan, and all your works and all your worship."
- They turn to the east, "the place of light" and paradise, and proclaim: "I believe in the Father, and in the Son, and in the Holy Spirit, and in one baptism of repentance."

John Chrysostom attests to a specific formula of allegiance to Christ: "And I enter into your service, O Christ." Likewise, the *Apostolic Constitutions* (7.41.3) adds a complete profession of baptismal faith, comparable to the Apostles' Creed (7.41.4-8).

Then came one or more anointings, according to the various churches. John Chrysostom gives an account of them:

> After that contract of renunciation and attachment . . . the priest anoints you on the forehead with the oil of the spirit and signs you (with the sign of the cross), saying: "So-and-so is anointed in the name of the Father, and of the Son, and of the Holy Spirit." . . . The enemy does not dare to look you in the face when he sees the lightning flash which leaps forth from it and blinds his eyes. . . .
>
> Next after this, in the full darkness of the night, [the priest] strips off your robe and, as if he were going to lead you into heaven itself by the ritual, he causes your whole body to be anointed with that olive oil of the Spirit, so that all your limbs may be fortified and unconquered by the darts which the adversary aims at you (*Baptismal Instruction* 2.2).[19]

For such anointings, the deaconesses took care of the women candidates (*Apostolic Constitutions* 3.16.4). We shall return to this. Authors of catecheses give diverse meanings to these rites: exorcism and purification, protection against the evil one, symbolism of the olive tree and its grafting (Rom 11:17-24, Christ is the olive tree on which the baptized are grafted), oil of the athletes, garment of immortality.

Then came baptism itself. The baptismal water had been prepared by a blessing, about which Ambrose gives the following commentary:

> It is not all water that heals, but that water heals which has the grace of Christ. The element is one thing, the working another. The water is the work, the working is of the Holy Spirit. Water does not heal, unless the Spirit has descended and consecrated that water. . . .
>
> As soon as the priest enters, he makes an exorcism over the element of water; afterwards he offers an invocation and a prayer, that the font may be consecrated, and the presence of the eternal Trinity may come down (*On the Sacraments* 1.15, 18).

In Jerusalem, the baptistry was located near the Anastasis, the Church of the Resurrection, built over the Holy Sepulchre. In this very proximity, Cyril found an added argument for his catechesis:

> You were led to the holy pool of Divine Baptism, as Christ was carried from the Cross to the Sepulchre which is before your eyes. And each of you was asked, whether he or she believed in the name of the Father, and of the Son, and of the Holy Spirit, and you made that saving confession, and descended three times into the water, and ascended again, here also, in a hidden manner, pointing by a figure at the three-days burial of Christ. . . . And at the self-same moment, you died and were born; and that Water of salvation was at once your grave and your mother. . . . (*Mystagogical Catechesis* 2.4).

The baptismal immersion was followed by several rites, among them those already practiced in the preceding period, as we have mentioned. For Milan, Ambrose speaks of an anointing with myron (perfumed oil) by the bishop, the washing of the neophytes' feet, the clothing with white garments, and the conferring of the "spiritual seal." As for Cyril of

Jerusalem, he alludes to the white garb and comments upon the anointing with myron, which was a symbol of the coming of the Holy Spirit, and was applied first on the forehead, then on the ears, nostrils, and chest.

John Chrysostom reports the recitation of the Our Father and the kiss of peace between faithful and neophytes, but he does not mention a post-baptismal anointing. Theodore of Mopsuestia is equally silent on this but briefly mentions the rite of the white garments and the signing of the forehead with a cross. The *Apostolic Constitutions*, however, make provision for an anointing with myron, but without specifying any relation to the gift of the Holy Spirit; and it speaks of the praying of the Our Father after baptism:

> After this [the post-baptismal anointing] let [the newly baptized] stand up and pray the prayer which the Lord taught us. Of necessity, the one who is risen again ought to stand up and pray, because the one that is raised stands upright. Let [the newly baptized], therefore, who has been dead with Christ, and is raised up with him, stand up. But let this one pray turned towards the east. . . . But let this one pray in these terms after the preceding prayer, saying: "O God Almighty, the Father of your Christ, your only begotten Son, give me a body undefiled, a pure heart, a watchful mind, a knowledge without error, and the presence of your Holy Spirit, that I may be founded in the truth and have full assurance of the same, through your Christ, through whom glory be to you, in the Holy Spirit, for ever. Amen" (7.45.1-3).

**Evolution of the Liturgy of Baptism.** From the fifth century on, the number of adult candidates for baptism diminished whereas the number of infant baptisms increased. The churches continued to use the same ceremonial of baptism, which had been designed for adults but could also be employed for children. A few adaptations were introduced. We find an example of these in a Roman sacramentary, the *Gelasian*, where in the organization of Lent, the following is specified for the *Traditio Symboli*:

> *Before saying the Creed, you will proceed, using these terms:*
> Dearly beloved, you who are about to receive the sacrament of baptism, . . . learn with attentive hearts the Creed and

what we transmit to you as we have received it; write it down, not on any corruptible matter, but on the pages of your hearts. . . .

> *After this, the acolyte takes one of the children, a little boy, and holds him in his left arm, places his [right] hand on his head. The priest asks:* In what tongue do they confess our Lord Jesus Christ? *The acolyte answers:* In Greek. *The priest continues:* Proclaim their faith as they profess it.
> *And the acolyte proclaims the Creed in Greek, while holding his hand on the child's head, speaking in these words* . . . [the Nicene Creed follows, in Greek].
> Dear brothers [and sisters], you have heard the Creed in Greek; listen to it also in Latin.
> *And you say:* In what tongue do they confess our Lord Jesus Christ? *He answers:* In Latin. —Proclaim their faith as they profess it.
> *Holding his hand on the child's head, the acolyte proclaims the Creed in these words* . . . [the Nicene Creed follows, in Latin] (Gelasian Sacramentary 1.35).

The rites which theologians have identified as constitutive of baptism, confirmation, and the Eucharist, formed one single celebration in ancient times. This is still the case today, even for the baptism of children, in the Eastern churches. On the other hand, in the West, if confirmation and the Eucharist were dissociated from baptism, it was for practical reasons. When the bishop was the sole minister of confirmation and in charge of extensive territories, he could not travel here and there immediately after every baptism. So the persons to be confirmed were grouped and presented to the bishop whenever he visited. However, certain eucharistic practices still remained in use, at least until the twelfth century, during the celebration of the baptism of children.

## Ministries and Ordinations

In the *Apostolic Constitutions*, the ceremonial of ordination contains the laying on of hands and the prayer, with epiclesis of the Holy Spirit, not only for bishops (8.4-5), presbyters (8.16), and deacons (8.17-18)—which was already the case in the *Apostolic Tradition*—but also for deaconesses (8.19-20), sub-

deacons (8.21), and readers (8.22). For the episcopal ordination, the participation of three bishops is required, except in
urgent cases; the consent of the local community is voiced in
the course of the ceremony; and the deacons hold the gospel
book over the candidate's head.

The communities spoken of in this document are important because of their numbers; they avail themselves of many
ministries which allow for the smooth functioning of assemblies and liturgical celebrations. The bishop's ministry is at the
center of the life of the local community and of all its institutions. This is demonstrated by the use of revealing titles:
shepherd, high priest, mediator, teacher, prophet, presider,
physician. It is he who normally presides over the liturgical assembly. He is assisted by presbyters, or priests, who form a
council around him and are in charge of teaching and can also
preside at the celebrations in place of the absent bishop, as
well as convene the assemblies in the neighborhoods of large
cities or in the country. Bishops and presbyters assume the
priestly ministry.

For their part, deacons perform a ministry of service in the
liturgical functions, but also in all forms of the pastoral, charitable, penitential, and economic activities of the communities.
They are helped by subordinate ministries (formerly called
"minor orders"). Their helpers are first of all the deaconesses,
who minister to women in diverse circumstances, in particular in the anointings at baptism; but they also serve women
who are sick or in stressful situations. Subdeacons assist deacons. The ministries of reader, cantor, and doorkeeper are self-
explanatory: they are in charge of the readings, singing, and
guarding of the doors during liturgical celebrations. Certain
churches also instituted exorcists, who worked within the
framework of the catechumenate, and acolytes for certain
functions in the service of the Eucharist, as we indicated above
when speaking of the church of Rome (see p. 84).

We also know the usages proper to Rome through descriptions contained in the documents called *Ordines Romani*.
Ordinations were held during the Sunday vigils of the weeks of
fast (Ember Days). For ordinations to the episcopacy, presbyterate, and diaconate, the ceremonial featured the presentation

of the candidate, the intercession of the whole assembly, the laying on of hands followed by the ordination prayer, the kiss of peace given to the ordinand and exchanged with him by those in the same clerical rank, and the participation of the ordinand in the Eucharist in the capacity of his new ministry.

The ordination of the pope (at that time the elect was a member of the Roman clergy) was to be held with the participation of three bishops of the district, and the rite of ordination demanded that the gospel book be placed on the head of the elect. In contrast, for the ordination of the bishops of his district, the pope alone conducted the ordination by laying his hand on the ordinand.

In Rome, the ordination to the three orders of reader, acolyte, and subdeacon essentially consisted in the candidates' entering into the functions of their ministries. The readers were young men for whom their fathers had provided an education and whom, on completion of their studies, they presented to the pope. The pope had them read during the vigils, and if the candidates' abilities were sufficient, he accepted them with a short blessing. For admission to the order of acolyte, the pope gave the candidates, during Communion, the linen satchel destined for the bread made Eucharist which was to be carried to the neighborhood churches (the rite of the *fermentum*). This rite was accompanied by a short blessing. The ordination of the subdeacons followed that of the acolytes during Communion and consisted in the presentation of the cup to the candidates with the same blessing as that given the acolytes.

A ritual from southern Gaul, incorporated into a Romano-Germanic compilation of the tenth century, proposed another ceremonial for admittance to the orders of doorkeeper, reader, exorcist, acolyte, and subdeacon. The main rite, identical for all five orders, consisted in the presentation of the instruments corresponding to each of these ministries: keys; lectionary; book of exorcisms; candlestick, with candle, and cruets; and sacred vessels.

The notion of liturgical ministry has evolved throughout the centuries according to the importance given to the different functions of this ministry and according to the various circumstances of the communities. In the fourth century, the emphasis on the ministry of the word is still very strong, as the following exhortation to bishops shows:

> You, therefore, O bishops, are to your people priests and Levites, ministering to the holy tabernacle, the holy Catholic Church, who stand at the altar of the Lord your God, and offer to God reasonable and unbloody sacrifices through Jesus the great High Priest. You are to the laity prophets, rulers, governors, and kings; the mediators between God and God's faithful people, who receive and declare God's word, well acquainted with the Scriptures. You are the voice of God and witnesses of God's will (*Apostolic Constitutions* 2.25.7).[20]

But later on, when the liturgical ceremonial greatly developed, the priestly aspect of the liturgical ministries was stressed, often by being compared to the liturgical institutions described in the Bible and to the Old Testament priesthood. The trend is already perceptible in the writings of Dionysius the Areopagite; his presentation of the bishop has been summarized in the following terms:

> As an instrument of purification, illumination, and perfection, (the "hierarch") must embody the highest perfection and the most radiant purity. He must not tarry among realities that scatter [his attention] and among occupations that divide [his single-mindedness]. If he must, of necessity, spread God's gifts over all the hierarchic orders and, so to say, come down into the domain of the multiplicity throughout which these gifts are diffused, he must immediately return to the divine principle which divinizes and unifies him. It is in this permanent communion with God that he acquires the true knowledge and the eminent holiness that render him also divine.[21]

We can appreciate the evolution that has taken place since the church orders of the first centuries, which, to the contrary, asked bishops to take an interest in all the realities of their communities. After the Peace of the Church, bishops and clergy enjoyed a personal status in the Empire; this brought to memory both the Old Testament institutions, including the exclusive status of the priestly class, and the social standing of pagan priesthoods.

## Marriage, a Family Ceremony

Prevented from accepting an invitation to a wedding in about 385, Bishop Gregory Nazianzen sent a letter of apology containing the following words:

> Let others call on the Loves since a wedding celebration warrants such playfulness. Let them describe the beauty of the bride; vying with one another, let them exalt the grace of the bridegroom and strew the bridal chamber with speeches and flowers at the same time. As for me, I want to sing you my wedding poem: the Lord bless you from Zion [Ps 128:5], ground your marriage in harmony, and may you see your children and grandchildren [Ps 128:6]. . . . This is what I would have wished you, had I been present, and what I wish you now. As for the rest, take care of it yourself, and let the father crown the bride and groom, as he has wished. For here is what we have decided when we attend weddings: to the fathers belongs the crowning, to us the prayers—and prayers, I know, are not hindered by distance (*Letter 231*).[22]

From this letter, it seems we can deduce that the presence of a minister of the community was not judged necessary for a Christian marriage. Prevented from attending, Gregory gives no thought to finding a substitute. In the way of rite, he mentions that of the crowning only to say that he prefers to leave it to the father of the family, according to custom.

Christians adopted marriage rites inherited from the surrounding cultures: joining of hands, giving of the veil, blessing, and crowning. They judged that the marriage bond was tied by none other than God, in an invisible manner. Iconographic witnesses reveal this by showing Christ holding the place of the father, head of the household. This evolution continued in the churches, and later on, in order to make manifest this action of God, ministers (bishops and presbyters) replaced the fathers as presiders of marriage rites.

In the ninth century, in the church of Rome, according to a letter of Pope Nicholas I (November 13, 866), the engagement ceremony was still a strictly familial practice; mutual consent was expressed and the dowry and ring were presented. In contradistinction, the marriage itself took place in church during the Eucharist. The couple received the blessing and the

veil, and a crowning took place when the couple came out
the church. But these rites were not obligatory. On the oth
hand, in the Byzantine church, the Quinisext Synod (691–6⁹
imposed the obligation to have the marriage ceremoɩ
presided over by a priest.

### The Reconciliation of Penitents

Two letters of Pope Innocent I, written in 405 and 416, gi
us an account of the difficulties caused by the reconciliation
sinners:

> How must we deal with those who after baptism ha.ᴢ
> consistently yielded to carnal pleasures and who at the end of
> their lives ask for both penance and reconciliation? There are
> two courses of action that can be followed towards them: one—
> ancient—very severe; the other—more recent—more lenient,
> through indulgence. According to the old custom, in the case
> mentioned above, one granted penance, but not Communion.
> We must be aware that in the remote past, persecutions were
> frequent, and Communion was rightly denied, lest a too easily
> obtained peace encourage the faithful, being assured of gaining
> reconciliation, to fall deeper into apostasy. Penance was
> granted them in order not to refuse them everything. . . . But
> once our Lord gave back peace to the churches and the terror
> passed, it was decided to grant Communion to the dying—to
> serve as a viaticum, thanks to the divine mercy, for those at the
> point of death—in order not to give the impression of imitating
> the harshness and rigor of Novatian, the heretic who denied
> the possibility of forgiveness. Therefore, Communion will be
> granted along with penance to those at the point of death
> (*Letter to Exuperius*, p. 169).[23]
>
> As for those who, either for grave sins or for lesser ones,
> are doing penance, one must, in the case of the persons in good
> health, reconcile them on the Thursday before Easter, according
> to the custom of the Roman church. As regards the appraisal of
> the gravity of their sins, it is up to the bishop or presbyter, who
> should also take into account the sinners' weeping and tears of
> repentance. It belongs to them to grant reconciliation when they
> are assured that the expiation is satisfactory. However, if some-
> one falls sick and is at death's door, he or she must be reconciled
> before Paschal Time, for fear that he or she depart from this
> world deprived of Communion (*Letter to Decentius*, pp. 29–31).

The penitential institution, spoken of in these two letters, was fully organized after the persecutions. Three steps are discernible:

1. *Entrance into penance.* This was presided over by the bishop or, in Rome, by the priest in charge of a neighborhood church. The rituals included a laying on of hands, then the clothing of the penitent with a coarse garment, the distinctive sign of the class of penitents. The community took part in this ceremony by praying and, as in the case of the catechumens, by verifying the quality of the penitents' conversion. In Rome, Ash Wednesday, the beginning of Lent, had become the traditional day for entering into penance. Theologians have long debated what kind of admission of guilt took place in this public ritual. Of course, the sinner recognized his or her sin, but this in no way implied a public confession, much to the contrary: for instance, Pope Leo the Great (d. 461) reminded people that it was forbidden to publicly read the list of sins; the confession had to be made in private. However, in many cases, the sin was known to all.

Only "sin that is mortal" (1 John 5:16) was subject to this penitential institution, in particular, idolatry, homicide, adultery, and fornication. "Everyday sins" were thought to be remitted through good works like almsgiving, prayer, the recitation of the Our Father, fasting, and so on.

2. *Duration of penitential time.* This was comparable to the catechumenate: it was meant to produce a profound conversion of the whole being and be recognizable by a change in outward behavior. The length of this phase varied with the gravity of the sin.

3. *Reconciliation.* What we have here is essentially a laying on of hands accompanied by a prayer. As one of the excerpts quoted above mentioned, in Rome, the reconciliation took place on Holy Thursday evening in order to associate the reconciled penitents with the paschal Eucharist and joy.

This reconciliation process was granted only once: if the reconciled penitent fell into sin again, the community did not feel itself capable of vouching for God's pardon a second time. For this reason, in order to prevent a grave relapse, authorities continued to impose a penitential regimen on penitents, complete with prohibitions, to the end of their days; these persons were bound to observe total continence, were barred from certain public functions and certain trades, were forbidden to sue anyone in a court of law, and, of course, were denied access to ministries.

These rigorous measures were the cause of serious pastoral problems from the fifth century on: to avoid being subjected one day to these prohibitions, the catechumens hesitated to ask for baptism and delayed it until their deathbed. As a result, this penitential institution was progressively abandoned: pastors kept the young persons away from it to avoid condemning them to a life of penance for the rest of their days; married people could submit themselves to it only with their spouses' consent, since the condition of penitent entailed complete continence; certain social positions were incompatible with the condition of penitent.

Whereas the West was going through a period of instability because of the fall of the Empire and the devastation resulting from the invasions—a background hardly favorable to the concerted development of institutions—the Christian East was adopting a more therapeutic approach in its pastoral care of penitents. The penance imposed on sinners was considered not a punishment, but a remedy aiming at curing penitents of their evil tendencies. The penitential period comprised several degrees in order of decreasing severity. Thus, Basil the Great writes concerning the murderer:

> He who has committed voluntary murder and afterwards has repented shall not partake of the Blessed Sacrament for twenty years. And the twenty years shall be divided thus in his case. For four years he ought to weep as a penitent of the first degree, standing outside the door of the house of prayer and asking the faithful who enter to pray for him, confessing his transgression. And after the four years he will be received among the hearers and for five years will go out with them. Then for seven years he will go out, praying with those in the rank of prostrates. For four years he will only stand with the faithful, but will not receive Holy Communion. However after these have been completed he will partake of the sacraments (*Letter 217*).[24]

The progression described concerns participation in the assemblies. From one step to the other, penitents are allowed to be present for a longer time: during the first phase, they are completely excluded and must remain at the door; then they are admitted only for the readings and must go out at the same time as the "hearers," that is, pagans interested in the faith, but not yet accepted into the catechumenate. During the following two phases, they are sent out respectively after a prayer of intercession and after the general intercessions. The organization of this graduated penance is already attested by Canons 11, 12, and 14 of the Council of Nicaea in 325.

The therapeutic forms of the confession of sins developed especially within monastic communities as early as the end of the fourth century. The spiritual guide was not necessarily a priest, and the penances imposed were considered a medicine and probation or verification in the framework of the community.

It was also within the monastic milieux that a new penitential practice developed in the West in the course of the seventh century: the tariffed penance found in the *Penitentials,* manuals listing the penances to be imposed for different sins. The monks who came from Ireland and England to evangelize the Continent spread these practices as far as Aquitaine and northern Italy. This new form of forgiveness met with immediate success in the West because the ancient forms of penance had become impracticable because of their severity.

Now, the tariffed penance offered a possibility of reconciliation without the burden of interdicts. It could be repeated: sinners could have recourse to it without any limit. It was secret: everything took place between penitent and confessor, not within the whole assembly. Penitents confessed their sins, and they received penances according to the "tariffs" listed in the penitential manuals in use. The penances for several faults could be added together. Once these had been satisfied, penitents came back to ask for absolution.

This penitential system led to certain abuses. Since the total of the several penances could be very heavy (for example, years of fasting), commutations came to be accepted: a penance could be replaced by another done by the penitent in person or by a third party. One could compensate for days of fast with prayers, almsgiving, the celebration of Masses—subject to monetary stipend—a pilgrimage, participation in a crusade. Indulgences derive from these practices.

## The Oil of the Sick

The letter of Pope Innocent I to Decentius supplies clear information on the oil of the sick. The pope was commenting on the passage from James' Letter (5:14-15) which speaks of this anointing of the sick with oil in the name of the Lord:

> There is no doubt that this text applies to faithful persons who are sick, to those who can be anointed with the holy oil of unction. This oil is blessed by the bishop and can be used not only by those who are ordained priests, but by all Christians who have the power to do the anointing when either they themselves or their relatives are afflicted by disease and the need is urgent (*Letter to Decentius*, p. 31).

When the pope specifies that he is speaking of sick persons who are believers, he does so because this unction cannot be given to catechumens. He also says in the same letter that penitents are similarly excluded.

## Liturgies for Martyrs and the Dead

According to funeral traditions already mentioned (see p. 59), the family and friends of the deceased person gathered at the grave side, not only on the day of burial (*depositio*), but also at certain other fixed dates. These meetings entailed forms of funerary meals, called *refrigerium*, where portions were reserved for the dead person, whose participation was signified by one empty place. Christians adopted these customs; communities assembled for such celebrations in honor of martyrs, and families in memory of their own deceased members. Pastors sought to suppress certain abuses, as is shown by an episode Augustine reported on the occasion of the stay of his mother, Monica, in Milan during the time of Bishop Ambrose.

> My mother had brought meal and bread and wine to certain oratories built to the memory of saints, as was her custom in

Africa. But the sacristan prevented her. . . . But when my mother brought her basket with those accustomed dainties—of which she meant to eat a little and give away the rest—she never allowed herself more than one small cup diluted to her sober palate. . . . And if there were many oratories of departed saints to be honoured in that way, she took round with her the same cup to be used in each place: and this, not only diluted with water but by now very lukewarm, she would share with others present in small sips, for her concern was with piety and not with the pleasure of the wine.

But when she found that the custom was forbidden by so famous a preacher and so pious a bishop even to those who used it soberly, lest it might be an occasion of gluttony to heavier drinkers; and because in any event these funeral feasts in honour of our parents in the faith were too much like the superstitions of the heathens, she abandoned the practice quite willingly. In place of her basket filled with the fruits of the earth, she learned to offer at the shrines of the martyrs a breast full of prayers purer than any such gifts. Thus she was able to give what she could to the needy; and the communion of the Lord's body was celebrated where the martyrs had been immolated and crowned in the likeness of His Passion (*Confessions* 6.2).

The *Apostolic Constitutions* have also preserved in the same section several rulings on this topic: gatherings at the tomb, funerary meals, abuses to avoid (drunkenness), and required prayers (8.41-44). Here is an excerpt:

Let the third day of the departed be celebrated with psalms, and readings, and prayers, on account of him who rose in three days; and let the ninth day be celebrated for the comfort of the bereaved as well as the remembrance of the departed, and the thirtieth day according to the ancient pattern, for so did the people lament Moses, and the year's mind. And let alms be given to the poor out of the departed's goods, for a memorial of the departed (8.42.1-5).

In another section, the same document records, with some additions, the ruling from the *Didascalia*, already quoted (see p. 59), on the same topic:

Assemble in the cemeteries, arranging the reading of the sacred books, and singing for the martyrs who have fallen asleep, and for all the saints from the beginning of the world, and for your brothers and sisters that are asleep in the Lord; and offer the acceptable Eucharist, the figure of the royal body of Christ, in your churches and cemeteries, and at the funerals of those who have fallen asleep accompany them with singing, if they were faithful in the Lord (*Apostolic Constitutions* 6.30.2).

According to Roman regulations, burial grounds were set wholly apart from the city. The martyrs' graves, and therefore the churches built above them, were situated outside the walls. The veneration of relics originally was done by direct contact: people came to touch the tomb, and a system was arranged to allow access to the tomb (the *confessio*, described on p. 76). The faithful took away as relics pieces of cloth or oil that had touched the holy body.

The discovery of St. Stephen's body, in 415, was the beginning of the spread of relics taken from the bones themselves. Later on, because of the insecurity resulting from the barbarian invasions, the remains of the saints which laid in the cemeteries outside the cities were transported into urban churches.

### Feasts and Calendars

Around 377, while speaking about the paschal solemnities, Epiphanius, bishop of Salamis (Cyprus), mentioned several traditions he had observed in the churches. Certain churches held daily assemblies from the ninth hour (3:00 in the afternoon) until evening during the first six days of the Great Week, as they had already done during the whole of Lent. Other churches celebrated only two vigils: the first from the evening of Holy Thursday to the dawn of Good Friday, the second during the paschal vigil. Still others had only one assembly, either on Holy Thursday at the sixth hour (noon) or on Easter Sunday at dawn.

During the same period, the *Apostolic Constitutions* recorded the existence of two calendars of yearly feasts. The first one (5.13-20) complemented the elements taken from the *Didascalia* (see pp. 60–61), indicating the date and the meaning of each feast:

- the Nativity, on December 25;
- the Epiphany, a manifestation of Christ's divinity, on January 6;

- the fast of forty days (Lent), as a commemoration of the life and teaching of Christ; the people fast every week from Monday to Friday;
- the Great Week of the Pasch (or Holy Week), whose six days, including Holy Saturday, are fast days;
- Easter, whose date is fixed on the Sunday following the full moon after the Spring equinox;
- the Sunday on the octave of Easter, according to the gospel of the appearance to Thomas;
- the Ascension, forty days after Easter, on a Thursday;
- the coming of the Holy Spirit, fifty days after Easter;
- there follow one week of festivities and one week of fast;
- a reminder of the weekly fast, observed the year around, on Wednesday and Friday, except during the Fifty Days, or Pentecost (Paschal Time according to our present terminology).

The second list of feasts (8.33) indicates on what days masters must free their slaves in order to allow them to participate in the Christian assemblies: Saturday and Sunday, the Great Week and the week following (Paschal Week), Ascension, Pentecost, Nativity, Epiphany-Baptism of Christ, feasts of apostles, feasts of St. Stephen and the other martyrs.

These two calendars already exhibit a great chronological faithfulness in the commemoration of the events of the Lord's life. But Christian feasts are not mere anniversaries, as the meaning given to the Epiphany shows: what is celebrated on this day is the manifestation of Christ's divinity, explained by the theophany at his baptism, without the text's even alluding to the episode of the magi. However, these calendars say nothing about what forms the celebration of these feasts took.

On the other hand, for Jerusalem, Egeria's narrative supplies a wealth of information on the ceremonial of each feast. It is true that the church of Jerusalem was in a unique situation. The local community, the monks, and the pilgrims sought the places that Jesus, the apostles, and, before them, the patri-

archs, the prophets, and the kings had marked with their im-
print. The gospel chronology was used as a foundation to
read, in the places and at the dates specified, the stories of the
events of Christ's life. These events were the nativity and
epiphany, the presentation in the Temple; the phases of the
passion, with the entry into Jerusalem, the Last Supper, the
agony, the veneration of the cross at Golgotha, and the vigil in
expectation of the resurrection; then, after Easter Sunday, the
Sunday of Thomas and the gift of the Holy Spirit with, on the
same day, the memorial of the ascension. From Jerusalem, pilgrims carried these cycles of feasts to the churches of East and
West.

Other witnesses also show that at the same period, the
churches celebrated the solemnities that have formed the liturgical calendar. Thus, Basil the Great revealed, as if in passing,
the meaning of the Fifty Days of Easter: they are the unfolding
of Easter Day.

> The entire season of Pentecost is likewise a reminder of the res-
> urrection we expect in the age to come. If we count that one
> day, the first of days, and then multiply it seven times seven,
> we will have completed the seven weeks of the holy Pentecost,
> and the season ends on the same day it began (Sunday) with
> fifty days having elapsed. Therefore this season is an image of
> eternity, since it begins and ends at the same point, like a circle
> (*On the Holy Spirit* 27.66).

## Conclusion: A Golden Age for the Liturgy

As has been said all along in this chapter, the Peace of the
Church fostered the development of all liturgical institutions:
what had been only a germ in apostolic times had the opportunity to unfold. However, within this golden age lasting several centuries, it is possible to distinguish several phases.
Thus, the period of stabilization, in the fourth and fifth centuries, was marked by the rapid growth of communities, a
consequence of massive conversions. The catechumenal and
baptismal institutions developed quickly to answer the need
to welcome adult converts. But after the fifth century, the populations of the Roman Empire having for the most part become Christian, adult baptisms grew rare. The catechumenate

was no longer much in demand, and certain of its rites sub-
sisted only as vestiges, for instance, the formulas for the dismissal of catechumens in the course of regular celebrations,
even when there were no longer any catechumens in the assemblies.

In the opposite direction, other liturgical institutions—
those destined to nurture the flowering of communities and
Christian life—still continued to develop: the ceremonial of
the eucharistic liturgy and of the daily assemblies, penitential
institutions, and so on. At the same time, the attention of
thinkers and preachers, no longer primarily involved with
catechumenal preparation, turned increasingly to the interpretation of and commentary on the eucharistic celebration and
the feasts of the liturgical calendar.

As far as rituals are concerned, by the eighth century, the
essentials had been established, and the innovations of the following centuries could affect only secondary or peripheral aspects: development of entrance rites, addition of prayers and
songs, decoration of the sanctuary, and so on. Nevertheless,
important developments characterize the following centuries,
but they bear not so much on the organization of the rituals as
on the manner in which each period utilizes them and under-
stands the liturgy.

Chapter 5

# Christendom:
# The Conversion of Nations
# and the Administration of the
# Common People

In spite of the recognition of Christianity as the official religion, the prosperity of churches was never unlimited. Without doubt, the communities grew and were able to develop their institutions, but the political situation underwent profound upheavals between the time of Constantine and the end of the Middle Ages. The Byzantine Empire preserved a relative stability until the fifteenth century, but only at its center because in the course of the centuries, its frontiers shrank gradually, to the point of comprising only the territories surrounding Constantinople. As for the West, from the fifth century on, it was devastated by successive invasions and regained a certain stability only under Charlemagne's reign.

In 452, Attila had invaded Italy. In 455, it was the turn of the Vandals. In 493, Theodoric established a Gothic kingdom. From 530 to 555, the Byzantine Empire undertook to reconquer part of the former western territories. In 568, the Lombards invaded northern Italy. And the turmoil continued. As a result of the invasions, the territory of the former Western Empire had been fragmented into a multitude of realms, whose rulers the barbarian chieftains—Ostrogoths, Visigoths, Burgundians, Vandals, Alemanni, Franks, and so on—had become. Urban civilization had greatly suffered from these events because of looting; the economy had returned to being principally rural, concentrated in vast domains where country parishes were established.

After the collapse of the civil institutions of the Roman Empire, it was through religious institutions, episcopal houses and monasteries, that the—now Christianized—cultural heritage of antiquity was preserved. In the northernmost part of the former Western Empire, where Roman civilization and Christianity were less firmly entrenched than in the southern provinces, Irish monks undertook a vast campaign of evangelization with the creation of an important network of monasteries, radiating from Luxeuil in eastern France into the valleys of the Moselle and the Rhine, to the shores of Lake Constance, to St. Gall in Switzerland, even to northern Italy.

## The Carolingian Renaissance
## and Its Effects on Christian Institutions

After the dissolution of the Merovingian kingdoms, the successors of Charles Martel, Pepin the Short (751–768) and Charlemagne (768–814), reorganized the entire territory which was under their rule. It was both a reform and a restoration. The new masters of the West had before their eyes a real model, from which they wanted to distance themselves, all the while copying it; this model was the Byzantine Empire, a Christian empire in which the political power deemed itself equally competent in the religious domain. Pepin the Short, then Charlemagne became the protectors of Christian Rome, exposed to renewed Lombard invasions, against which the Byzantine Empire had not been able to extend a helping hand. This resulted in the church of Rome becoming estranged from Constantinople and placing itself under the tutelage of the Western political rulers by recognizing their legitimacy through the royal coronation and the imperial consecration (of Charlemagne on Christmas Day of the year 800).

From that time on, the bonds between the two churches, East and West, continued to weaken more and more. The two sides followed different historical courses. So, in the following pages, the comparisons between the Roman liturgy and the Byzantine liturgy will be sparse, and we shall limit ourselves to the description of the institutions of the Western churches.

A mosaic of diverse populations, the new Western Empire realized its unity through Christianity:

The profession of one faith was what truly held the Carolingian enterprise together. Princes and bishops closely collaborated—in spite of some divergences of opinion—to gather all people of the Empire into the Catholic and Roman faith, the only bond of unity strong enough to overcome the other differences and give rise to common mental attitudes. . . . In the Carolingian princes' eyes, baptism, the entrance into the Catholic Church whose head, Rome, was situated within the Empire, meant integration into the Christian people of which they were the rulers. In the minds of both princes and prelates, the identification of the Empire and the Christian people reached completion during the ninth century. This identification tended to give this part of Western Europe its own personality which its leaders and thinkers opposed to Islam, the paganism of the northern regions—a paganism which they were fighting—and Byzantine Orthodoxy—which they both despised and feared. This is why we can speak of a Carolingian Christendom.[1]

The conversion of the peoples was decided by their leaders; the same practice obtained in the eastern lands (present Eastern Europe), where the nations close to Byzantium had converted to Christianity because their princes willed it. The Christianization of these masses could be effected only by missionaries or by an "imported" clergy; the following generations supplied the recruits for the local clergy and monasteries:

Carolingian society continued to recognize the distinctions of personal status inherited from antiquity. . . . The universal administration of baptism had not resulted in total and rapid social uniformity. But besides all these distinctions and these juridical, political, and social groups, a new frontier of religious origin created a division between clerics and laypeople. This had never existed in Greco-Roman paganism, where priesthood—barring very rare exceptions—did not entail a privileged social status. Through special rights and duties and through a distinct way of life, a very high barrier between cleric and lay was erected and would become a principle.[2]

The strict institutional separation between clerics and laypeople should not be erroneously projected into antiquity; it comes from the Carolingian church, and this explains why it is peculiar to the Catholic church. The Byzantine church does not know it under the same form.

Not only baptism, but all liturgical institutions were pressed into service as means for the unification of the Carolingian Empire. Up to that time, the churches continued to follow the traditions of their provinces or their metropolises. However, some liturgical books were in circulation in episcopal houses and monasteries, at least since the eighth century: catalogues of biblical pericopes for the readings, collections of Mass formularies, groupings of sung pieces. The Roman origin of certain of these books has been ascertained; other books reflect the customs of the Gallic churches. The most important among these collections, the one which has been called "Old Gelasian Sacramentary"—although it cannot be ascribed to Pope Gelasius (492–496)—has both Roman formularies and Gallican pieces. Now, Charlemagne and his ecclesiastic advisers undertook to make liturgical practices uniform by imposing the same books on all the churches.

## The Importation of Roman Liturgical Books

Charlemagne asked Pope Hadrian (772–795) to send him a purely Roman sacramentary (collection of Mass formularies). The request was granted only after a certain delay. The pope sent a version of the sacramentary called "Gregorian"—although it was put together after the time of Gregory the Great (590–604). The book was placed in the library of the royal palace in Aachen in order to serve as a model. It was copied immediately by many scribes and diffused throughout the Carolingian Empire.

In its central part, the original nucleus, the Gregorian Sacramentary contains the formularies used in the stational liturgy: Masses for the time of Christmas and Epiphany and for the Easter cycle, together with Lent and Pentecost. This stational liturgy concerned the celebrations that gathered the church of Rome, by turns, in the great basilicas and in the neighborhood churches. The pre-Vatican II missals still bear the mark of this origin in their calendar, for example, First Sunday of Lent, Station at St. John Lateran. In the Gregorian Sacramentary, the moveable cycle (around Easter) and the feasts of the saints are intermingled, whereas in the Old Gelasian Sacramentary (mentioned just above), they are classified separately into two books.

In the version which reached Aachen, the Roman collection had already been enlarged. But even in this state, it was insufficient since it had been compiled only for use at the stational liturgy. It therefore was submitted to a second edition, corrected and augmented through the labors of St. Benedict of Aniane, who added an important supplement; this is called the "Hadrianum with Supplement." Benedict explained his purpose in a long introduction that enlightens us on the reception that these books met with. Here are some excerpts:

> Because there exist other [formularies] necessary to the practice of the holy Church, but omitted [in Roman book], we have deemed it worthwhile to collect them as flowers blooming in the meadows, to gather them, and once corrected and given titles, to incorporate them in this volume in order for the reader to find here all that we consider necessary in our day, although we do find the greatest part of this also in other sacramentaries. . . .
>
> We beseech those who like these [formularies] collected by us without any pretense, but with utmost care and fervent love, not to forget our labor, but rather to give thanks with us to the author of all gifts.
>
> Let those who see our work as superfluous and of no use to them be content with [the book received from Rome]—which they cannot reject without depriving themselves—and leave the rest to those who are interested in it and plan to use it with piety.
>
> We have collected these [formularies] not for ungrateful [people] and disdainful minds, but for interested and pious persons: thus, those who appreciate this work will be able to find in it the means for fulfilling their vows and celebrating the divine worship with dignity in a manner pleasing [to God]. May the discriminating reader know that we have included in this work only what especially qualified and learned persons have carefully produced. We have gathered numerous [formularies] from many sources in order to serve the purposes of the greatest number.
>
> Another thing, we ask those who find pleasure in the prefaces we have placed at the end of the volume to receive and sing them with love. We have a request to address to two kinds of readers: on the one hand, those who understand them but do

not appreciate them and, on the other hand, those who would like them but do not understand them; we ask them not to use them and not to sing them.

We also have added episcopal blessings to be recited over the people as well as the [formulary] of the ordinations to minor orders, which are missing from the book [received from Rome].

As a consequence, we implore all you who will take this volume in hand, in order to read or copy it, to address prayers to the Lord for me, who have endeavored to collect and correct all this for the benefit of the greatest number. We also ask you to copy the book with care so that its text may charm the ears of the learned and prevent the simple from going astray, for as the blessed Jerome says, there is no use correcting a book if the copyists do not care to respect the corrections.[3]

Following a practice usual among grammarians of the Carolingian period, Benedict of Aniane had corrected the book received from Rome. He had borrowed from other sacramentaries or had himself composed the necessary complements: Mass formularies, prefaces, and blessings over the people. We have here a direct testimony to the circulation of liturgical books: the collection, imported by Charlemagne, was added to others already in general use.

As a consequence, Benedict foresaw several attitudes on the part of those who would see this work: certain people would have none of it, which indicates that Charlemagne's reform was not received without reluctance; others would want only the sacramentary that had come from Rome, without Benedict's additions; finally, still others would welcome the whole thing, to the compiler's greatest satisfaction.

The importation of Roman books and their diffusion throughout the whole Empire, on Charlemagne's orders, signaled in the West the demise of the oral tradition in the liturgical domain. Up until then, each church was the depository of its tradition, which it attributed to its founders, which it transmitted from generation to generation and scrupulously respected. By imposing a written work, which had come from elsewhere, Charlemagne and his advisers made the book the obligatory reference and the norm for future times. Thus, local oral traditions were progressively replaced by a written law, codified and supposedly composed by authoritative persons, inasmuch as Roman books were considered the work of the best-known popes, in particular Gregory the Great.

## Evolution of the Books of the Roman Liturgy

In the beginning, the liturgical collections were varied in their purpose, their titles, and their realization. At first, they were put together in view of certain ministries exercised in the assembly. The first were the catalogues of the biblical pericopes to be read, the Bible being the only book indispensable for the celebration. Then, the very texts of the readings, excerpted from the Bible, were assembled—arranged according to the calendar—in lectionaries: the epistle book for the subdeacon, the gospel book for the deacon.

The prayers and instructions were gathered in the sacramentaries, and the sung pieces destined for the schola (select choir), in the antiphonaries and graduals. The formularies for baptisms, ordinations, reconciliation of penitents, and blessings were written at their places in the annual cycle, on the corresponding days (the catechumenate during Lent, the reconciliation on Holy Thursday, baptism at the paschal vigil, and so on).

Beginning in the tenth and eleventh centuries, people began to regroup the elements of the different ministries into complete books, organized by celebrations: in the altar missal were gathered the readings, the texts of the sung pieces, and the prayers for the Mass, components that used to be distributed in four books: epistle book, gospel book, sacramentary, and antiphonal. The multiplication of private Masses (see pp. 126–127) seems to have strongly influenced this development: as the priests were now performing all functions by themselves, a single book was made available to them, containing, besides the texts pertaining to them, what in the assembly was the charge of the readers and cantors.

Other books resulted from similar reorganizations. The pontifical contained a selection of formularies for the celebrations presided over by the bishop (ordinations, solemn reconciliation of penitents, dedication of churches, coronations, and so on). And from the fourteenth century on, rituals appeared; they were manuals destined for priests, with the liturgical texts they needed in their pastoral charge (baptism, marriage, anointing of the sick, blessings, and so on).

The interest Frankish clerics took in the Roman liturgy led them to go and observe the celebrations in Rome itself and to write *ordines* (*ordo* in the singular): accounts of the order in which they were carried out. The diffusion of these *ordines* was aimed at helping the users to understand the sacramentaries which habitually contain only the texts of prayers. The contents of certain of these accounts were adapted to the circumstances of churches other than that of Rome; other accounts describe non-Roman traditions.

Basing themselves on these different books, which are as many witnesses to the liturgical practices in force between the sixth and the ninth century, historians have attempted to reconstruct the ceremonial in use in Rome at that time, and also those of the churches of the Carolingian Empire. The task is a demanding one, and many uncertainties remain because the books containing the formularies, or the lists of readings, are collections without "directions for use" and provide scant data on how they were actually employed; also, the information offered by the *ordines* do not cover the entire field of the liturgy.

The Roman books had collected traditions relative to the practices of the churches of the city of Rome. The churches of the peoples governed by Pepin the Short and Charlemagne were differently organized because they were implanted in primarily rural regions. However, in their fervor, certain bishops transposed into their churches customs born of the Roman forms of pastoral care and sometimes not suitable for other places. Thus, Chrodegang (d. 766) introduced the stational liturgy in Metz. Another example of aberration: liturgical collections at times juxtaposed several formulas or rituals intended for the same celebration; and instead of choosing, people ended up reciting and performing everything, which gave rise to repetitions and doublets. Thus, in the old missal, for the blessing of ashes at the beginning of Lent, the priest consecutively said four prayers with identical contents.

In this movement of unification, Roman liturgical books, which at the outset were practical manuals, became normative documents whose every prescription was faithfully executed. Liturgy was becoming a codified worship; pastoral care was no longer its inspiration.

## Stabilization of the Liturgy in the Roman Church

After the Roman books had been adopted, the churches of the Carolingian Empire mixed certain of their own traditions with those borrowed from the church of Rome. This produced hybrid rituals, Romano-Frankish, as for ordinations, whose ceremonial has preserved rites which were Gallican in origin (introductory directions, rituals of investiture, presentation of the instruments corresponding to each ministry, and so on). Later on, these same rituals were adopted by the church of the city of Rome at the time of the Gregorian reform (Gregory VII, 1073–1085), under the influence of popes of Germanic descent. Thus, the circle was closed: the liturgical books that had left Rome, taking along the usages proper to that city, returned, bringing back hybrid rituals compiled in the Frankish churches. After this, the rituals of the Roman church did not evolve much: they were stabilized in their principal forms. In contrast, the evolution would bear on the way they were understood and put into practice.

Chapter 6

# Stability, Fixity, and Restorations of the Roman Liturgy from the Twelfth Century to Vatican II

The Carolingian Renaissance was followed by a new period of turmoil in the eleventh century. Then from the twelfth century on, the West at last knew a longer era of stability, which favored the spreading of urban civilization, the rapid rise of law, the flowering of universities and schools (among them, those of theology), the advancement of the arts (Romanesque and Gothic periods), and so on. None of the political, social, or cultural upheavals that followed this medieval period provoked important transformations of the rites. Rather, it would be more accurate to speak of a slow drift in the implementation of the liturgy.

As early as the eleventh century, liturgical unity had been elevated to the level of an ecclesiological principle by the Gregorian reform, promoted by Pope Gregory VII. From that time on, the popes attributed to themselves a liturgical competence for all the churches. At the level of practice, liturgical unity was understood as uniformity. This was easy to see in the struggle against heresies, when Roman customs were imposed to replace local practices that had become the object of suspicion, as happened in Spain in the eleventh century. The Catholic reforms of the sixteenth century led to similar solutions.

Indeed, the Council of Trent (1563–1614) undertook the correction of the abuses denounced by the Reformers concerning the way of celebrating and understanding the Mass (see pp. 128–129). But the decisions taken in the liturgical domain did not produce any modifications either in the organization of the rituals or in the exclusive use of the Latin language, whereas the Protestant Reformers had profoundly reworked the eucharistic ceremonial and had adopted vernacular languages.

Owing to the centralization, fixity, and uniformization of rituals, the period extending from the twelfth century to Vatican II is of limited interest for the history of the fundamental liturgical institutions. If one wants to study the structure of the ecclesial celebrations and their evolution, one observes only secondary evolutions, like the multiplication of private prayers said by priests during Mass; the insertion of genuflections, signs of the cross, and movements to and fro at the altar; and so on. These centuries are of greater interest to the history of piety, spirituality, religious sentiment, and also—under the heading of history of liturgy—to the history of the rites of a local church or of a religious order.

It is thanks to Vatican II that the liturgy has again been recognized in its true dimensions, as the realization of the Christian mystery, and that it has recaptured its strength of expression. But before this reform may bear all its fruits, much time and a transformation of minds will be necessary.

## The Eclipse of the Liturgical Assembly

We have mentioned above (see pp. 114–116) the importance of the Carolingian Renaissance. A historian, casting an impartial eye on Western Christianity in the eighth century, was led to write:

> Like Judaism, Christianity instituted a priestly class for itself. Indispensable mediators between believers and God, bishops and priests are much more than the leaders of prayer: alone, they baptize; alone, they consecrate the bread and the wine of the sacrifice in buildings defined and blessed by them alone.[1]

Let us hasten to quote the clarification offered by Vatican II:

> Let [all] be persuaded that the Church reveals herself most clearly when a full complement of God's holy people, united in prayer and in a common liturgical service (especially the

Eucharist), exercise a thorough and active participation at the very altar . . . (*Constitution on the Liturgy*, no. 41).[2]

There is no hint of a priestly class in the texts of Vatican II; but nine centuries before, the feudal society acknowledged that it was organized in three orders: "Some pray, others fight, others work." Such a concept made of clerics professionals of worship, and as a consequence, the liturgical assembly became a clergy gathering. This development reached the church of Rome itself: the pontifical liturgy moved from the Lateran basilica, open to all the people, to the private papal chapel, which was then recognized as a model to imitate, and became a clerical liturgy.

Because of this clerical monopoly of liturgical activity, the ministries that had been instituted to foster the participation of the people lost their purpose; and according to the perceptions of the time, the liturgical ministry was concentrated in the sole priesthood. As a consequence, the ancient orders of doorkeeper, reader, exorcist, and acolyte were no longer exercised in the service of the liturgy. However, they did not disappear altogether; they became merely preparatory steps to the diaconate and the priesthood. The practice even developed of holding formal ordinations or "institutions" which were not directed to the service of the assembly. This usage continues in force and one still institutes "reader" candidates, the majority of whom have already performed this function for a long time. The duties of the ancient lower ministries have been assigned to subordinate officials like sacristans, beadles, vergers, ushers, and in convents and monasteries, to lay brothers.

The functions of deacon and subdeacon have endured, sometimes even those of acolyte (reduced to the role of altar servant) and reader, in churches where the clergy is numerous, as well as in monasteries, convents, and collegiate churches (that is, belonging to chapters of canons). But it also happened that priests were charged with performing the ritual functions of deacons and subdeacons. Traces of this were recognizable in the past at funeral services when, in everyday language, one spoke of "three-priest Masses." These were not yet the concelebrations reestablished by Vatican II, but services in which two of the priests wore the liturgical vestments of deacon and subdeacon.

Clerics and monks took care of the daily celebrations: Mass and the different offices that mark the successive hours of the day (up to eight offices per day). The colleges of canons were assisted by lay persons: cantors, instrumentalists, beadles, and so on. Together, they were the professionals of the liturgy and their livelihood was guaranteed for that purpose. The daily office of the hours was a rather heavy task, especially for clerics engaged in pastoral duties; consequently, in the thirteenth century, the private recitation of the office was allowed for clerics who for legitimate motives were unable to attend the choral office. This necessitated the creation of appropriate books, called "breviaries," in which were collected for private use the material divided between the large books used by several persons in the choirs of monks and canons.

From the sixteenth century on, new congregations even rejected the choral office. Thus the Jesuits, approved in 1540:

> His [Ignatius'] sole purpose in obstinately refusing to let his men assume the *obligation* of daily common office in choir was exactly the same as his reason for refusing to accept the permanent cure [that is, care] of souls; both require fixed residence and the obligation to be in certain places at certain times, and that would hinder the mobility and freedom Ignatius wished for the apostolic endeavors he envisaged as the vocation of his men.[3]

Toward the end of the Middle Ages, liturgy had become a ceremonial. Meanwhile, canon law had elaborated a doctrine of the Church-society, which caused a shift in the way of perceiving the Church. Indeed, throughout the first millennium, when one spoke of the Church, one spontaneously thought of the liturgical assembly since it is the liturgical assembly that renders the Church visible and perceptible in its fundamental reality, as people of God and body of Christ. But from the twelfth century on, this visibility shifted toward the Church as society, with its hierarchy (the pope, the bishops, the clerics), its orders, its institutions, its authority over the temporal power, and so on.

## From the Ecclesial Celebration to the Private Mass

About the ninth century, a certain practice became general, a practice that would have momentous repercussions on the understanding of the liturgy and on the way theologies would approach problems. We are speaking of the private Mass, said by a lone priest without the presence of an assembly. What took place there was not a modification of the rites of the Mass, but their application to a practice at odds with the very soul of the liturgy: the Eucharist, summit and center of the life of the Church, was celebrated without an ecclesial community.

The same Mass formulary used for the solemn celebration, with deacon and subdeacon, was transposed to the private celebration of one priest assisted by one servant; and the pieces that supposed the singing of the schola or the common response of the assembly were recited, some by the priest, some by his servant, and sometimes by the priest alone.

The spread of the private Mass seems connected to the system of graduated penances allowing commutations which made it possible to replace fast days with the celebration of Masses (see pp. 106–107). At the same time, the concern for the ransoming of deceased sinners in view of their eternal salvation led people to have Masses celebrated for the souls of the dead. Now, the practice of private Masses allowed for the multiplication of celebrations with a minimum of personnel. However, in order to answer a strong demand, the number of priests was considerably increased, particularly in monasteries, whereas the contemplative life per se did not entail priestly ordination. The same thing happened with the new religious orders of the Middle Ages: among the mendicant orders (Franciscans, Dominicans, and so on), priests were soon in the majority.

In the parish clergy, there was also an increase in the number of priests. Estimates have been made for a few dioceses or cities at the end of the Middle Ages:

> In the diocese of Geneva, where 140,000 people lived, one counts 1,400 clerics, whether priests or not, that is, one percent of the population. The city of Geneva alone, with 10,000 inhabitants, had twenty priests. The other priests were assigned to rural parishes at the rate of one pastor and two curates each. In

other words, each priest was in charge of some 50 families, that is about 250 persons. In England, the clerics represented two percent of the population.[4]

By requesting private Masses for one's penance or for the dead, the absent donor considered the priest his or her delegate. The Roman Eucharistic Prayer (Canon of the Mass, now Eucharistic Prayer Number 1) bears traces of this evolution of outlook. In its primitive form, the commemoration of the living was couched in the following terms: "Remember your servants and maidservants and all those here present . . . who offer you a sacrifice of praise. . . ." A significant addition has transformed the text: "Remember your servants and maidservants. . . . We offer to you for them, or they offer to you. . . ." In this context, the priest acts in the name of the faithful, no longer in common with them since they are absent and have made him their delegate by means of a monetary offering.

The practice of private Masses also led to the insertion of the priest's multiple personal prayers, called "apologies" because they confess the unworthiness of the celebrant and appeal to the divine mercy. Then, still other formulas were added to accompany every gesture: when putting on the priestly vestments, preparing the gifts, moving about, and so on. The liturgical reform of the Council of Trent retained only a small number of these formulas, certain of which have remained and appear in the present-day missal (prayer of the deacon or priest before the gospel, silent invocation before Communion).

The manner of celebrating private Mass contaminated even the solemn celebration. Beginning in the twelfth century, there appeared a practice contrary to the spirit of the liturgy: even when the schola was doing the singing and when the subdeacon and deacon proclaimed the readings, the priest recited in a low voice the text of the chants and similarly read the readings for himself.

In addition, the practice of celebrating private Masses gave rise to excesses. First, because of their multiplication—for instance, one thousand Masses would be said for a deceased person—it became necessary to forbid priests to celebrate more than thirty Masses per day. Second, to satisfy the considerable demand for Masses, some priests resorted to the "twofold or triple Mass": they repeated two or three times the first part of the Mass up to the preface, but said the canon (Eucharistic Prayer) only once, while receiving two or three stipends. The Reformers of the sixteenth century denounced these abuses and the Council of Trent took measures to put an end to them.

### The Missal of Pope Pius V

Pius V implemented the decrees of the Council of Trent by publishing the *Missale Romanum* (Roman Missal) in 1570. This was not a new ceremonial but the restoration of ancient traditions:

> One could be led to believe by the bull of Pius V who recommended the missal, that the work of the commission had been very thorough and really well documented; in reality, the work was far from being so. . . . In fact—probably due to the urgency of the needed measures—the missal, called "of Pius V," was only the reedition, with rare corrections, of that used by the Roman Curia in 1474. Thus, what some call "the missal of Pius V" is in reality so only because this pope promulgated it; but it existed a full century before this promulgation. This missal was imposed on the universal church. However . . . the dioceses and religious orders which had been celebrating a particular liturgy for over two hundred years were allowed to continue with it. . . . In fact, it was easier, especially for small dioceses, to accept the proposed reform. Nevertheless, the Dominicans and the dioceses of Milan and Lyon, for instance, kept on using their own liturgies, in spite of the imposition of the universal missal, and this with the full agreement of the authorities.[5]

The Curia, or pontifical administration, had become a clerical college, already important during the sojourn of the papacy in Avignon (fourteenth century). It had created its own liturgical books which, by reason of the prestige of Roman authority, came to be regarded as models by some local churches and some religious orders; they even became, like the missal, normative books imposed upon what was called "the universal church," in fact, the totality of the dioceses of the Latin church, as distinct from the Eastern churches.

The liturgical reforms of the Council of Trent no doubt made the practice of Christian worship much more sound, but they did not allow for the active participation of the Christian people in the liturgy, which Vatican II proclaimed four centuries later. Various local reforms were undertaken in the seventeenth and eighteenth centuries, but they were short-lived.

*Let us add here a note on the place of the celebrant at the altar.* The practice of the Mass "facing the people," started at the time of Vatican II, was a reaction against the most frequent form of the Mass, that celebrated by a priest at the altar, reciting both the readings and the prayers with his back turned to the assembly. The Mass facing the people was intended to reestablish a real dialogue. But the liturgists were not yet sufficiently aware that in ancient times, the dialogue took place in many ways, that the orientation of the whole assembly (see p. 75) did not impede the participation of the faithful, that the readings were proclaimed facing the people, and that several ministers, the deacon in particular, played their part in guiding the whole assembly.

### From the Celebration to the Administration of the Sacraments

The function of the liturgy was twofold: to render the worship due God and to insure the sanctification of Christians. Now, these two functions are inextricably linked by the mysterious presence of Christ to his Church in the liturgical celebration: Jesus leads us by his Spirit in the praise of the Father, and the presence of the Spirit in Christ's ecclesial body is precisely the source of holiness. But from the Middle Ages on, the two functions were distinguished and this distinction supplied an explanation for the practices then current: the clergy rendered worship to God, which could be done without the people, and it insured the believers' sanctification through rites, including the sacraments. Thus, worship was for God and, in a certain measure, for the benefit of Christians. The vocabulary testifies to this evolution: the point was not so much to "celebrate" the sacraments with the faithful as to "administer" the sacraments to them.

If the Fourth Lateran Council (1225) prescribed confession at least once a year and Communion at least at Easter, it was because the mass of Christians held themselves aloof from the eucharistic table. Historians have collected telling testimonies on this subject. For instance, in Saint-Georges Church of Haguenau in Alsace, the records show only 2,300 Communions of the faithful for the whole year 1462, but in contrast, during the same period, there was a yearly purchase of 3,000 large hosts for the priests saying Masses.[6]

As Communions became rare, other forms of participation in the Eucharist arose, in particular contemplation. In order to satisfy the desire "to see the host," everything that contributed to seeing it was fostered, but not without risks, as can be attested by the debates between theologians of the time on the exact moment of the consecration:

> As he gets ready to say the words of consecration over the host, which is still only bread, the priest . . . raises it to a moderate height at his chest. In the second half of the twelfth century, this gesture tends to become more emphatic. The not yet consecrated host is raised higher and higher in order to be seen by the people who, crowded behind the priest, adore the body of Christ. Soon it becomes evident that this gesture risks leading the faithful into the worst of sins, idolatry; indeed, there is a great danger that they adore what is still only bread. This gesture must be banned and the solemn elevation of the host must be allowed only after it is consecrated. But when does the consecration take place? [There follows a listing of the different responses of the theologians of the period.][7]

For centuries, the elementary pastoral teaching consisted in convincing the faithful that they must go to confession and Communion regularly. The Council of Trent did not say anything else. But in this context, the sacraments are seen as "means of communicating grace," and this by an individual approach without any mention of the ecclesial dimension. Communion is even dissociated from the eucharistic celebration and distributed outside Mass. Two examples illustrate well the mindset which these practices fostered. One is the *Spiritual Exercises* of St. Ignatius where, in regard to Mass, they treat only of Communion, but ignore the eucharistic celebration. The other is the solemn proclamation of indulgences in Rome, which was accompanied by the reading of the conditions necessary to gain the indulgences: confession and Communion were required, but there was no mention of the eucharistic celebration.

Through the administration of the sacraments, priests gave a framework to believers' Christian life: baptism, confession (reconciliation), and Communion, but also to the celebrations that in the early centuries most often remained within the family circle, marriage and anointing of the sick. During the eleventh century, as a reaction against a climate of violence and social anarchy, the Western churches contributed to the introduction into the formalities of marriage a greater respect for persons. Church legislation imposed a preliminary inquiry, entrusted to the priests, the public celebration of weddings—to guarantee the freedom of the woman's consent—and the reception of the nuptial blessing.

In this system, the priest assumed several functions: he presided at the celebration and gave the blessings, but he also acted as lawyer in order to verify whether the conditions of validity were fulfilled, and as "marrier" because it was he who gave away the bride to the bridegroom. This led some theologians to consider the priest as the minister of the sacrament of marriage. With time, the function of "marrier" was downplayed and the emphasis placed on mutual consent; thus, the couple's role was expressed in a clearer fashion. Numerous local rites had been adopted in the marriage celebration, but after the Tridentine reforms, very few of them were retained, in spite of the recommendations of the Council.

Similarly, the anointing of the sick progressively became more strictly regulated. Whereas, earlier, the faithful were allowed to apply the blessed oil themselves (see p. 107), from the tenth and eleventh centuries on, the anointings were done only by priests on the basis of James 5:14, and books of rituals were elaborated for this administration.

At weddings, the dialogue relating to the spouses' consent was said in the people's tongue, but all the other sacraments were administered in Latin. As a consequence, since the beneficiaries (except those who were educated) did not understand what was said, no effort was wasted on the adaptation of rites, and the ritual of the catechumens—barely modified—was used for infant baptisms.

## The Funeral Rites

The liturgical substratum of the funeral rites was relatively simple: it was made of Mass formularies, and the chanting of the psalms with antiphons (refrains) was borrowed from the Liturgy of the Hours. The development of the funeral rites consisted mainly in the repeated celebration of Masses for the dead and in the heavy emphasis on the setting and solemnization of the ritual: hangings, catafalques, altar servants, musical compositions with choirs and orchestras, and so on. The liturgical texts came from the old Roman books which had been imposed by the Carolingian reform. In the thirteenth century, a lengthy poetic composition, the *Dies irae*, was introduced before the gospel and has been a particularly fecund source of inspiration for musicians.

## The Calendar and Feasts

In the course of the centuries, the yearly calendar was unceasingly augmented by new feasts of saints. Feasts in honor of Mary already existed in the Roman books: Annunciation (March 25), Nativity (September 8), Presentation in the Temple (November 21), Dormition (August 15). But under the influence of the devotion to Mary in the Middle Ages, the feasts of the Christological cycle acquired more of a Marian coloration; for instance, the Presentation of Jesus in the Temple changed into the Purification of Mary. Throughout the centuries, the cycle of Marian feasts was further augmented with feasts connected to historical events, for example, since 1571, the feast of the Rosary, on October 7, commemorating the victory over the Turks at Lepanto; the commemoration of the first appearance of Mary to Bernadette at Lourdes, on February 11. Theme-feasts were also added: the Immaculate Heart of Mary, the Seven Dolors, the Holy Name of Mary.

In the same way, the calendar of saints' feasts (sanctorale) was constantly increased by the multiplication of feasts due to the canonization of new saints or to the transfer of relics and other anniversaries. On several occasions, the pontifical authority made some severe prunings in this calendar. The latest of these cuts was decided by Vatican II, whose main concern was to reestablish the preeminence of the Sunday celebration, which was often supplanted by feasts of saints.

## The Expansion of Devotions

Beginning with the Middle Ages, "divine worship" had become a collection of rites scrupulously executed to insure validity and sacramental efficacy. And then, the progress of printing and the centralizing action of the Roman Congregations further reinforced this liturgical fixity by circulating the official books and imposing them on all churches. The result was that there was no room for pastoral innovation. However, this was all the more necessary since the liturgy—because of the Latin language—remained closed to the Christian people. Therefore, it was outside official worship that movements of piety expressed themselves by creating what came to be called "devotions." These were so numerous and diverse that the history of Western piety is far richer than that of the liturgy during the same period. We shall briefly discuss this expansion of devotions in order to situate it in reference to the liturgy.

In parishes and churches of religious dedicated to pastoral care, these devotions invaded the whole field of personal piety and even sacramental practices. We give here a glimpse of this state of affairs; it concerns devotion to the person of Christ:

> At the end of the Middle Ages, religious life is lived, so to speak, on two levels, clearly distinct. The masses, especially in rural districts, practice a religion that is essentially demonstrative. Processions, pilgrimages, and the cult of relics occupy a place at least as important as the sacraments—irregularly received anyway—and prayer. . . . In the larger cities and around monasteries, a smaller number of Christians, laypeople as well as clerics, apply themselves to nurturing a more interior and more personal piety. . . . It is not required of Christians that they be knowledgeable and eloquent, but that they see, contemplate, meditate, and thus suffer in union with Christ. For the primary object of meditation is the suffering Christ.[8]

Let us mention at least two needs which the development of devotions satisfied. First, there is the need for a conscious religious expression. Christian prayer must be a dialogue personally assumed by believers. The whole biblical dynamism leads to the rejection of magical formulas and to the admission of only a comprehensible, conscious, and responsible expression in prayer (see Matt 6:7). Now, because of its exclusive use of the Latin language, the liturgy of the West did not allow laypeople to express themselves consciously in prayer; they were obliged to say words they did not understand. By contrast, devotions offered them prayers in their own tongue. Second, for the devout believer, prayer tends to occupy as completely as possible the whole field of activities and to be as continuous as possible in time. And devotions proposed practices that tended to achieve this goal: prayers or exercises for the different moments of the day and the diversity of occupations.

Now, it belongs to the very nature of liturgical institutions, to fulfill, in the spirit of Christ, these two needs. In fact, in the West during the first centuries, as long as the people understood Latin, the liturgy was able to nourish the dialogue of prayer and the personal relation to God. Moreover, as we saw above, Christian communities, having inherited from Judaism the traditions of prayers giving rhythm to the passage of time, held daily synaxes. In certain monastic centers, this extension of the liturgy over every moment of life had led the monks to lengthen or even double the Liturgy of the Hours by adding other offices in their desire to invest more time in prayer. The liturgy had the power of satisfactorily answering the call to prayer.

The expansion of devotions brought about the development of forms of meditation, for instance, those exercises which proposed methods for applying the mind and the imagination to such and such a mystery, in particular to the passion of the Lord. This is precisely what the liturgy abundantly supplied in the first centuries; and in later times, church iconography had continued to fulfill this need. But the shortening of the readings at Mass and their being kept in a learned language had destroyed this fine balance. It would have been enough to give back to the Liturgy of the Word its due place and to respect its spirit. However, from the eleventh century on, nobody gave any thought to this since the competent authorities had not permitted the use of vernaculars. One would have to wait until Vatican II decided to take such pastoral initiatives.

Originally destined for the faithful, certain devotions were substituted for liturgical institutions which, as a consequence, became the province of clerics. For daily prayer, the Angelus marked the three periods of the day, morning, noon, and evening; and the rosary replaced the main offices of the Liturgy of the Hours. In any case, the number of Hail Marys for the rosary, 150, was inspired by the number of psalms. However, one observes a certain imbalance, caused by the preponderance of a devotion to Mary that had become excessive and was too dependant on affectivity: the formulas addressed to Mary took the place of those addressed to God. It was the Our Father the *Didache* had asked believers to recite three times a day. But in the rosary, what a disproportion exists: at the end of its evolution, it retains only one Our Father for each decade.

Devotions should not be confused with the liturgy and can never replace it. In the past, such a thought never arose since devotions at least presupposed "sacramental practice" and were intended for the faithful. Now, devotions fundamentally differ from the liturgy in their origins, in the way they are structured, and in their forms of expression. Whereas the liturgy is the present celebration by Christ, in his Church, of the mystery of the New Covenant, devotions are personal prayers, and even if they are practiced in common, they never will be anything more than the juxtaposition of individual acts.

We must deplore the success of devotions because they invaded the whole of Catholic consciousness at the expense of the liturgy. Even though the latter officially continued to be celebrated, its meaning had been lost to the point that the liturgy was simply "the social form of the virtue of religion." Because this virtue consists in rendering worship to God, it was thought that this could be done privately or collectively. Traces of this imbalance remain even in books published in recent years: they mention sacraments but not liturgy. Only the

*Catechism of the Catholic Church* (1992) restores a certain equilibrium to this domain since it presents the sacraments in a chapter on the liturgy (nos. 1066–1206).

Vatican II has restored the teaching of liturgy in the formation of the clergy. We must recognize that this teaching was not given in a satisfactory way prior to the Council; we must also recognize that many bishops, still active in our day, studied for the priesthood before this reform. Did they get the opportunity to rethink their formation and to make their own the orientation urged by the Council, concerning the balance between liturgy and devotions?

## The Arrangement of Church Buildings

The arrangement of church buildings from the Gothic period on betrays the deviation of the Latin liturgy—which had become the province of clerics—and the invasion of devotions. This is visible first of all in the multiplication of churches and chapels and in the plan of the edifices destined for the choral liturgy of canons, monks, and religious. In many European cities, there are within short distances of one another churches built in the past for collegiate chapters of Dominicans, Recollets, Cordeliers, Carmelites, and so on. The sanctuary is noticeably lengthened, variably according to the number of the clerics, monks, or religious to be accommodated; these received stipends or were supported by the believers' piety. In this space reserved for the clergy, all the appointments for the celebrations were concentrated: altar; seats for the officiants; stalls for the canons, monks, or religious; lecterns for the readings; credences (tables for the objects necessary to the services).

In the twelfth century, the sanctuary was even isolated by a rood screen. This item was an excrescence of the ambos and pulpits destined for the readings and proclamations, as is still seen in the Church of Saint-Etienne-du-Mont in Paris. In most cases, the rood screen took the form of a gallery or even a wall giving access to the sanctuary only through a door, as can be seen in the cathedral of Albi, France. An altar was placed in front of the screen for the faithful in the nave. In this way, two parallel liturgies were performed, that of the clergy in the sanctuary (or chancel) and that of the people in the nave.

The multiplication of private Masses led to the setting up of secondary altars placed in lateral chapels along the nave and in apsidioles (small apses). The altars were fitted with illustrated retables, originally intended for the nurturing of the celebrant's piety by the evocation of Christ's mysteries. But, as time went on, the veneration of saints was abundantly expressed on these retables so that the phrase "to place on the altar" means to be canonized. To place someone on the altar means that he or she will have a statue or painting on an altar.

The theological debates on the Eucharist fostered the designing of containers destined for the reserved Eucharist: first, niches or cupboards set in the walls of the sanctuary, then, receptacles in the shape of delicately carved towers. After the reform of Trent, the container for the reserved Eucharist, that is, the tabernacle, was installed on the main altar, except in cathedral churches, where the ancient tradition was maintained and where the reserved Eucharist was kept in an auxiliary chapel.

Under the influence of reforming currents during the Middle Ages, in particular that of the orders of preachers who had undertaken the Christian formation of the people, pulpits were installed in the nave of the churches. Preaching gave rise to services independent of the eucharistic celebration and outside the sanctuary: invocation of the Holy Spirit, sermons, prayer in the form of litanies (still detectable in the old formula of Lenten sermons for instance).

As a consequence of the juxtaposition of offices and devotions, the appointments were duplicated, the spaces within a single church multiplied: sanctuary, chapels, side altars. Several offices could take place at the same time, and at the end of the Middle Ages, the recollection in those churches was not remarkable: people stood when they wanted, they chatted, and dogs were free to wander as they pleased. In the course of centuries, reforming movements regularly endeavored to restore calm and silence in churches.

Beginning with the Middle Ages, statues appeared in the Western churches. Up to then, iconography had been limited to mosaics and frescoes, or else to sculpture in low relief (Roman sarcophagi, tympanums of doors, and Romanesque capitals). But already at the end of the ninth century, relics were encased within statues (reliquary-statues), and progressively the statues themselves became the object of veneration, with or without relics.

Statuary developed considerably in the Catholic churches, in large part because of the veneration of saints. From collective representations, such as the sculptured groups of the annunciation, nativity, burial of Jesus, and so on, statuary changed to portrayals of individuals: every saint had his or her statue on an altar or on the walls and pillars of a church. As regards the purpose of these statues, the sculptured groups representing biblical mysteries could be professions of faith, making explicit one or another aspect of salvation. But what was the purpose of statues of saints displayed singly? The Baroque period favored exuberance, expressing the joy of living and a certain "triumphalism" on account of the victory of Catholic truth. But from the nineteenth century until Vatican II, statuary sunk into what is called "Saint-Sulpice art" (from the stores where this art is displayed, close to that church in Paris) or "Barclay Street art" (from the street in New York where numerous religious goods stores once stood). These mass-produced statues are too often made of low-quality material (plaster) and in a conventional and academic style, with expressionless features.

All this deterioration in the decoration of churches was connected with the excessive development of devotions and the loss of the meaning of the liturgy. In this context, the decisions of Vatican II are easily explained as urgent reforms prepared by movements of renewal that had denounced all the deviations affecting the practice of Christian worship and the organization of its setting.

# Conclusion

What distinguishes the Christian mystery from all other religious institutions is that Christians, called by the Risen Christ, gather every Sunday as a community. These assemblies are local realizations of the people of God; in them, the New Covenant is lived. The communities listen to the Word of God, follow Christ in the eternal offering of his love to the Father, and enter in communion with the Spirit of God, who sends them into the world as witnesses of the resurrection. Thus, the liturgy, starting from the Sunday Eucharist, is the center and source of the whole life of the churches.

If the New Covenant is eternal, the liturgical assemblies are nonetheless marked by time inasmuch as the churches are immersed in the world, which is that from which they grow and to which they address themselves. One may consider the historical variations in the manner of conducting liturgical celebrations with the eyes of faith and with pastoral concern.

The eyes of faith, intent on discovering the marvels worked by God in God's Church—and thus faithful to the spirit of the formulas of blessing—will recognize in the diverse adaptations of the liturgy the action of the Holy Spirit that guides pastors, as one preface proclaims:

> It is right to give [you] thanks and praise. . . .
> You are the eternal Shepherd
> who never leaves his flock untended.
> Through the apostles
> you watch over us and protect us always.
> You made them shepherds of the flock
> to share in the work of your Son,
> and from their place in heaven they guide us still. . . .[1]

This recognition of the action of the Holy Spirit corresponds to the invocations expressed in the prayers for the ordination of bishops, and more precisely in their epicleses. Indeed, they implore the coming of the Holy Spirit on the new bishop in order that he may "pasture God's flock." The charge of pastor entails the taking of initiatives, under the guidance of the Holy Spirit, to direct the institutions of the local church according to its vocation. This is admirably defined by Augustine in his recommendations concerning catechesis:

> With this love, then, set before you as an end to which you may refer all that you say, so give all your instructions that [the one] to whom you speak by hearing may believe, and by believing may hope, and by hoping may love (*First Catechetical Instruction* 4.8).

With these eyes of faith, one sees that the liturgy is pastoral. Through it, God convokes and guides God's people toward communion with God, that is to say, the New Covenant. This pastoral function has, in fact, stimulated creativity, as one can recognize by studying liturgical innovations in the course of history. Let us recall simply some of the achievements of the church of Rome. The development of the stational institution was the result of initiatives aiming at realizing and manifesting the unity between the "base communities" scattered throughout an extensive and loose urban fabric. Likewise, the institution of the weeks of fast called Ember Days seems to have been a way of Christianizing ancestral rites. Elsewhere, many other liturgical innovations have consisted in transforming local pre-Christian practices according to the spirit of the New Covenant.

But when the liturgy was hardened into unchangeable codes, the pastors were able to exercise their creativity only by producing substitutes for the liturgy: devotions, spiritual exercises, paraliturgies. The result of this was to unbalance the right functioning of the institutions and to obfuscate the central place of the liturgy in the Christian mystery.

Nowadays, since the action of Vatican II tends to restore the right equilibrium to Christian institutions by giving back to the liturgy the central place which is its due, a review of the past allows us to draw out the lessons of history and opens pastoral perspectives. Comparative studies have led to numerous suggestions. Here are some examples:

—*Repetition or variety in the formulation of liturgical prayers.* Recent practices have favored variety, offering a wealth of formularies to choose from. Conversely, some currents of piety (which also make recruits among the young) favor certain repetitive formulas: the same text, about fifty words long, is repeated scores of times. These options must be examined from the viewpoint of liturgical tradition, but also, as the progress of human sciences permits us to do, they must be evaluated from the viewpoint of communication within an assembly and of the personal memorization of the message of faith.

—*Song and psalmody.* Christian liturgical singing comes from psalmody (we think of Gregorian chant). Psalmody consisted in flexible melodies whose rhythms were not rigid and allowed the setting of biblical texts and liturgical compositions to music. By contrast, the adoption of modern melodies with their regular, almost mechanical rhythms imposes on the text set to music the constraint of the melodic mold. The result is that the form (with its number of feet and rhymes) dominates the content of the text and is an obstacle to the setting of biblical texts to music.

—*The Christian vocabulary and the formation of the relation to God.* In the churches of the Roman rite today, the religious vocabulary widely used by the Christian people derives in large part from the language of theological schools and has incorporated numerous Scholastic and post-Tridentine abstractions. At the same time, the language of the liturgy is mainly biblical, for the liturgy (signs, rites, symbols, and so on) is not primarily defined by philosophical or theological concepts but in terms of the economy of salvation. The language of the liturgy penetrates the spirit of believers by nurturing personal prayer, not just rational expression.

If history is the teacher of life, the eyes of Christian faith allow us to recognize in it as well the mysterious presence of God who, through the Spirit, guides God's people, the Body of Christ. And this happens, above all, in the liturgy.

# Notes

## Introduction

1. Georges Auzou, *De la servitude au service*, 2nd ed. (Paris: L'Orante, 1961) 81–82.

2. *Catechism of the Catholic Church* (Citta del Vaticano: Libreria editrice Vaticana, 1994) nos. 1066–1068. This reflects the *Constitution on the Liturgy*, no. 5.

3. Nicholas Cabasilas (Byzantine mystical writer of the fourteenth century), *The Life in Christ*, trans. Carmino J. deCatanzaro (Crestwood, N.Y.: St. Vladimir's Seminary Press, 1974) 110, 194.

4. This is the definition of "liturgy" in Peter Eicher, ed., *Dictionnaire de Théologie* (Paris: Cerf, 1988) 369.

## Chapter 1

1. Pierre Grelot, *La liturgie dans le Nouveau Testament* (Paris: Desclée de Brouwer, 1991) 34.

2. Basil the Great (ca. 329–379), *On the Holy Spirit*, trans. David Anderson (Crestwood, N.Y.: St. Vladimir's Seminary Press, 1980). Quotations are taken from this edition.

3. Cyprian (d. 258), *The Letters of St. Cyprian of Carthage*, vol. 3, trans. G. W. Clarke, Ancient Christian Writers 46 (New York: Newman Press, 1984).

4. Discussion of the theses in a note of Paul Galtier, S.J., *L'Eglise et la rémission des péchés aux premiers siècles*, 2nd ed. (Paris: Beauchesne, 1932) 219.

## Chapter 2

1. *Didache*, in Cyril C. Richardson, ed. and trans., *Early Christian Fathers*, Library of Christian Classics 1 (Philadelphia: Westminster Press, 1953). Quotations from the *Didache* are taken from this edition.

2. Pliny the Younger (61–ca. 113), *Letter 96,* in *The Letters of the Younger Pliny,* bk. 10, trans. Betty Radice (Baltimore, Md.: Penguin Books, 1963) 294.

3. See also 1 Cor 12:28-29; 1 Tim 3:1-13; 5:17.

## Chapter 3

1. Tertullian (ca. 160–ca. 225), in Willy Rordorf and André Schneider, trans., *L'évolution du concept de tradition dans l'Eglise ancienne,* Traditio christiana 5 (Bern: Peter Lang, 1982).

2. Geoffrey J. Cuming, trans., *Hippolytus: A Text for Students,* 2nd ed., Grove Liturgical Study 8 (Bramcote, England: Grove, 1987). All quotations from the *Apostolic Tradition* are taken from this edition.

3. Arthur Vööbus has edited and translated the Syriac *Didascalia* in *The Didascalia Apostolorum in Syriac,* Corpus Scriptorum Christianorum Orientalium 402, 408 (Louvain: CorpusSCO, 1979). Quotations are taken from this edition, referenced by chapter and page, for example, 12,130–131. A convenient compilation of liturgical passages is Sebastian Brock, ed. and trans., and Michael Vasey, ed., *The Liturgical Portions of the Didascalia,* Grove Liturgical Study 29 (Bramcote, England: Grove, 1982).

4. Ignatius (ca. 35–ca. 107), in Richardson, *Early Christian Fathers.* Quotations from Ignatius are taken from this edition.

5. Justin (ca. 100–ca. 165), in Richardson, *Early Christian Fathers.* All quotations from the *First Apology* are taken from this edition.

6. Eusebius, *Ecclesiastical History,* vol. 2: *Books 6–10,* trans. Roy J. Deferrari (New York: Fathers of the Church, 1955). Quotations from the *Ecclesiastical History* are taken from this edition.

7. *Martyrdom of Polycarp,* in Richardson, *Early Christian Fathers,* 17–18.

## Chapter 4

1. Cyril (315–ca. 386), *St. Cyril of Jerusalem's Lectures on the Christian Sacraments: The Protocatechesis and the Five Mystagogical Catecheses,* Frank L. Cross, ed. (Crestwood, N.Y.: St. Vladimir's Seminary Press, 1977). Quotations from the *Mystagogical Catecheses* are adapted from this edition.

2. Ambrose (ca. 339–397), *On the Sacraments and On the Mysteries,* ed. James H. Srawley, trans. Thomas L. Thompson (London: S.P.C.K., 1950). Quotations from *On the Sacraments* are adapted from this edition.

3. Robert Cabié, *La lettre du pape Innocent Ier à Décentius de Gubbio* (Louvain: Publications universitaires, 1973). Quotations from the *Letter to Decentius* are taken from this edition.

4. Maxwell E. Johnson, *The Prayers of Sarapion of Thmuis*, diss. (South Bend, Ind.: Notre Dame, 1992). Quotes from Sarapion are taken from this edition.

5. Pseudo-Dionysius, *The Complete Works*, trans. Colm Luibheid and Paul Rorem (New York: Paulist, 1987). Quotations from Pseudo-Dionysius are taken from this edition.

6. Egeria, *Egeria's Travels to the Holy Land*, trans. John Wilkinson (Jerusalem: Ariel Publishing House, 1981). Quotations from Egeria (also known as Etheria) are taken from this edition.

7. W. Jardine Grisbrooke, ed. and trans., *The Liturgical Portions of the Apostolic Constitutions: A Text for Students*, Grove Liturgical Studies 61 (Bramcote, England: Grove, 1990). Quotations from the *Apostolic Constitutions* are adapted from this edition.

8. Procopius (mid-6th century), *Procopius*, vol. 7: *Buildings*, trans. Henry B. Dewing and Glanville Downey, (Cambridge: Harvard University Press, 1953).

9. Theodore of Mopsuestia (ca. 350–428), *Homélies catéchétiques*, ed. Raymond Tonneau and Robert Devreesse (Rome: Biblioteca Apostolica Vaticana, 1949) 463.

10. According to the edition and translation of Louis Bouyer, *Eucharistie, théologie, et spiritualité de la prière eucharistique* (Paris: Desclée, 1966) [*Eucharist: Theology and Spirituality of the Eucharistic Prayer*, trans. Charles Underhill Quinn (Notre Dame, Ind.: Notre Dame University Press, 1968).]

11. René Marichal, *Premiers chrétiens de Russie: Introduction, choix et traduction des textes*, Chrétiens de tous les temps 16 (Paris: Cerf, 1966) 52–53.

12. Amalarius of Metz, *Liber officialis*, 3.18, in Robert Cabié, *Histoire de la messe* (Paris: Desclée, 1990) 65.

13. Nicholas Cabasilas, *A Commentary on the Divine Liturgy*, trans. J. M. Hussey and P. A. McNulty (London: S.P.C.K., 1960) 61–62.

14. Henryk Paprocki, *Le mystère de l'Eucharistie: Genèse et interprétation de la liturgie eucharistique byzantine* (Paris: Cerf, 1993) 409.

15. Eusebius of Caesarea, in Robert Taft, S. J., *The Liturgy of the Hours in East and West: The Origins of the Divine Office and Its Meaning for Today* (Collegeville, Minn.: The Liturgical Press, 1986) 33.

16. Basil the Great, bishop of Caesarea (ca. 330–379), in Benoit Gain, *L'Eglise de Cappadoce au IVe siècle d'après la correspondance de*

*Basile de Césarée (330–379),* (Rome: Pontificium Institutum Orientale, 1985) 171.

17. Augustine (354–430), *The Confessions of St. Augustine,* trans. Francis J. Sheed (New York: Sheed and Ward, 1943). All quotations from the *Confessions* are taken from this edition.

18. Augustine, *The First Catechetical Instruction,* trans. Joseph P. Christopher, Ancient Christian Writers 2 (Westminster, Md.: Newman Bookshop, 1946). All quotatons from the *First Catechetical Instruction* are taken from this edition.

19. John Chrysostom (ca. 347–407), *Baptismal Instructions,* trans. Paul W. Harkins (Westminster, Md.: Newman Press, 1963) 2.22.

20. Adapted from *Constitutions of the Holy Apostles,* in Alexander Roberts and James Donaldson, eds., *The Ante-Nicene Fathers* (New York: Charles Scribner's Sons, 1925) 7:409.

21. René Roques, *L'univers dionysien: Structure hiérarchique du monde selon le Pseudo-Denys* (Paris: Aubier, 1954) 182–183.

22. Gregory Nazianzen (329–389), *Letter to Eusebius,* in *The Fathers Speak,* trans. Georges A. Barrois (Crestwood, N.Y.: St. Vladimir's Seminary Press, 1986) 200.

23. Innocent I (pope, 402–417), *Letter to Exuperius of Toulouse,* in Cyrille Vogel, ed. and trans., *Le pécheur et la pénitence dans l'Eglise ancienne* (Paris: Cerf, 1966) 169.

24. Basil the Great, *Letters,* trans. Sister Agnes Clare Way, C.D.P., vol. 2: *Letters (186–368),* Fathers of the Church 13 (New York: Fathers of the Church, Inc., 1955) 108.

## Chapter 5

1. Jean Chélini, *L'aube du Moyen Age: Naissance de la chrétienté occidentale* (Paris: Picard, 1991) 44.

2. Ibid., 33.

3. Jean Deshusses, ed., *Le sacramentaire grégorien,* vol. 1, 2nd ed. (Fribourg, Switzerland: Editions universitaires, 1979) 351–353.

## Chapter 6

1. Michel Aubrun, *La paroisse en France: Des origines au XVème siècle* (Paris: Picard, 1986) 11.

2. Vatican Council II, *Documents of Vatican II,* ed. Walter M. Abbot (New York: Herder and Herder, 1966) 152.

3. Taft, *Liturgy of the Hours,* 293.

4. Aubrun, *La paroisse en France,* 159.

5. Adrien Nocent, O.S.B., *La célébration eucharistique avant et après saint Pie V* (Paris: Beauchesne, 1977) 44–45.

6. Francis Rapp, ed., *Histoire du diocèse de Strasbourg,* Histoire des diocèses de France 14 (Paris: Beauchesne, 1982) 71, 73.

7. Jean-Claude Schmitt, *La raison des gestes dans l'Occident médiéval* (Paris: Gallimard, 1990) 346.

8. Philippe Denis, *Le Christ étendard: L'Homme-Dieu au temps des réformes (1500–1565)* (Paris: Cerf, 1987) 16–17.

## Conclusion

1. Present-day *Roman Missal*, Preface of the Apostles (as in the old *Missale Romanum*).

# Selected Bibliography

*Authors and works quoted in the text*

Ambrose. *On the Sacraments and On the Mysteries.* Ed. James H. Srawley. Trans. Thomas L. Thompson. London: S.P.C.K., 1950.

Aubrun, Michel. *La paroisse en France: Des origines au XVème siècle.* Paris: Picard, 1986.

Augustine. *The Confessions of St. Augustine.* Trans. Francis J. Sheed. New York: Sheed and Ward, 1943.

_____. *The First Catechetical Instruction.* Trans. Joseph P. Christopher. Ancient Christian Writers 2. Westminster, Md.: Newman Bookshop, 1946.

Auzou, Georges. *De la servitude au service,* 2nd ed. Paris: L'Orante, 1961.

Barrois, Georges A., trans. *The Fathers Speak.* Crestwood, N.Y.: St. Vladimir's Seminary Press, 1986.

Basil the Great. *Letters.* 2 vols. Trans. Sister Agnes Clare Way, C.D.P. Fathers of the Church 13, 28. New York: Fathers of the Church, Inc., 1951–1955.

_____. *On the Holy Spirit.* Trans. David Anderson. Crestwood, N.Y.: St. Vladimir's Seminary Press, 1980.

Bouyer, Louis. *Eucharistie, théologie, et spiritualité de la prière eucharistique.* Paris: Desclée, 1966. [*Eucharist: Theology and Spirituality of the Eucharistic Prayer.* Trans. Charles Underhill Quinn. Notre Dame, Ind.: Notre Dame University Press, 1968.]

Brock, Sebastian, ed. and trans, and Michael Vasey, ed. *The Liturgical Portions of the Didascalia.* Grove Liturgical Study 29. Bramcote, England: Grove, 1982.

Cabasilas, Nicholas. *A Commentary on the Divine Liturgy.* Trans. J. M. Hussey and P. A. McNulty. London: S.P.C.K., 1960.

*The Life in Christ.* Trans. Carmino J. deCatanzaro. Crestwood, N.Y.: St. Vladimir's Seminary Press, 1974.

Cabié, Robert. *Histoire de la messe.* Paris: Desclée, 1990.

_____. *La lettre du pape Innocent Ier à Décentius de Gubbio.* Louvain: Publications universitaires, 1973.

*Catechism of the Catholic Church.* Citta del Vaticano: Libreria editrice Vaticana, 1994.

Chélini, Jean. *L'aube du Moyen Age: Naissance de la chrétienté occidentale.* Paris: Picard, 1991.

Chrysostom, John. *Baptismal Instructions.* Trans. Paul W. Harkins. Westminster, Md.: Newman Press, 1963.

Cuming, Geoffrey J., trans. *Hippolytus: A Text for Students,* 2nd ed. Grove Liturgical Study 8. Bramcote, England: Grove, 1987.

Cyprian. *The Letters of St. Cyprian of Carthage.* 4 vols. Trans. G. W. Clarke. Ancient Christian Writers 43–44, 46–47. New York: Newman Press, 1984–1989.

Cyril. *St. Cyril of Jerusalem's Lectures on the Christian Sacraments: The Protocatechesis and the Five Mystagogical Catecheses.* Ed. Frank L. Cross. Crestwood, N.Y.: St. Vladimir's Seminary Press, 1977.

Denis, Philippe. *Le Christ étendard: L'Homme-Dieu au temps des réformes (1500–1565).* Paris: Cerf, 1987.

Deshusses, Jean, ed. *Le sacramentaire grégorien.* 3 vols. Spicilegium Friburgense 16, 24, 28. Fribourg, Switzerland: Editions universitaires, 1971–1982.

Egeria. *Egeria's Travels to the Holy Land.* Trans. John Wilkinson. Jerusalem: Ariel Publishing House, 1981.

Eicher, Peter, ed. *Dictionnaire de Théologie.* Paris: Cerf, 1988.

Eusebius Pamphili. *Ecclesiastical History.* 2 vols. Trans. Roy J. Deferrari. New York: Fathers of the Church, 1953–1955.

Gain, Benoit. *L'Eglise de Cappadoce au IVe siècle d'après la correspondance de Basile de Césarée (330–379).* Rome: Pontificium Institutum Orientale, 1985.

Galtier, Paul, S.J. *L'Eglise et la rémission des péchés aux premiers siècles,* 2nd ed. Paris: Beauchesne, 1932.

Grelot, Pierre. *La liturgie dans le Nouveau Testament.* Paris: Desclée de Brouwer, 1991.

Grisbrooke, W. Jardine, ed. and trans. *The Liturgical Portions of the Apostolic Constitutions: A Text for Students.* Grove Liturgical Studies 61. Bramcote, England: Grove, 1990.

Johnson, Maxwell E. *The Prayers of Sarapion of Thmuis.* Dissertation. South Bend, Ind.: Notre Dame, 1992.

Marichal, René. *Premiers chrétiens de Russie: Introduction, choix et traduction des textes.* Chrétiens de tous les temps 16. Paris: Cerf, 1966.

Nocent, Adrien, O.S.B. *La célébration eucharistique avant et après saint Pie V.* Paris: Beauchesne, 1977.

Paprocki, Henryk. *Le mystère de l'Eucharistie: Genèse et interprétation de la liturgie eucharistique byzantine*. Paris: Cerf, 1993.

Pliny the Younger. *The Letters of the Younger Pliny*. Trans. Betty Radice. Fathers of the Church 19, 29. Baltimore, Md.: Penguin Books, 1963.

Procopius. *Procopius*. Trans. Henry B. Dewing and Glanville Downey. 7 vols. Loeb Classical Library. Cambridge: Harvard University Press, 1953–1961.

Pseudo-Dionysius. *The Complete Works*. Trans. Colm Luibheid and Paul Rorem. New York: Paulist, 1987.

Rapp, Francis, ed. *Histoire du diocèse de Strasbourg*. Histoire des diocèses de France 14. Paris: Beauchesne, 1982.

Richardson, Cyril C., ed. and trans. *Early Christian Fathers*. Library of Christian Classics 1. Philadelphia: Westminster Press, 1953.

Roberts, Alexander, and James Donaldson, eds. *The Ante-Nicene Fathers*. Vol. 7. New York: Charles Scribner's Sons, 1925.

Roques, René. *L'univers dionysien: Structure hiérarchique du monde selon le Pseudo-Denys*. Paris: Aubier, 1954.

Rordorf, Willy, and André Schneider, trans. *L'évolution du concept de tradition dans l'Eglise ancienne*. Traditio christiana 5. Bern: Peter Lang, 1982.

Schmitt, Jean-Claude. *La raison des gestes dans l'Occident médiéval*. Paris: Gallimard, 1990.

Taft, Robert, S. J. *The Liturgy of the Hours in East and West: The Origins of the Divine Office and Its Meaning for Today*. Collegeville, Minn.: The Liturgical Press, 1986.

Theodore of Mopsuestia. *Homélies catéchétiques*. Ed. Raymond Tonneau and Robert Devreesse. Rome: Biblioteca Apostolica Vaticana, 1949.

Vatican Council II. *The Documents of Vatican II*. Ed. Walter M. Abbot. New York: Herder and Herder, 1966.

Vogel, Cyrille, ed. and trans. *Le pécheur et la pénitence dans l'Eglise ancienne*. Paris: Cerf, 1966.

Vööbus, Arthur, ed. and trans. *The Didascalia Apostolorum in Syriac*. Corpus Scriptorum Christianorum Orientalium 402, 408. Louvain: CorpusSCO, 1979.

*Books on the history of the liturgy and sacraments*

Danielou, Jean. *The Bible and the Liturgy*. Liturgical Studies 3. Notre Dame, Ind.: Notre Dame University Press, 1956.

Deiss, Lucien. *God's Word and God's People*. Trans. Matthew J. O'Connell. Collegeville, Minn.: The Liturgical Press, 1976.

Kucharek, Casimir. *The Sacramental Mysteries: A Byzantine Approach*. Allendale, N.J.: Alleluia Press, 1976.

Jungmann, Josef Andreas, S.J. *The Early Liturgy, to the Time of Gregory the Great*. Trans. Francis A. Brunner. Liturgical Studies 6. Notre Dame, Ind.: Notre Dame University Press, 1959.

Martimort, Aimé-Georges, and others. *The Church at Prayer*, new ed. 4 vols. Trans. Matthew J. O'Connell. Collegeville, Minn.: The Liturgical Press, 1986–1987.

Martos, Joseph. *Doors to the Sacred: A Historical Introduction to Sacraments in the Catholic Church*. Garden City, N.Y.: Doubleday, 1981.

Oesterley, William Oscar Emil. *The Jewish Background of the Christian Liturgy*. Oxford: Clarendon Press, 1925.

Wegman, Herman A. J. *Christian Worship in East and West: A Study Guide to Liturgical History*. Trans. Gordon W. Lathrop. New York: Pueblo, 1985.

### Collections of Documents

Deiss, Lucien, ed. *Early Sources of the Liturgy*, 2nd ed. Trans. Benet Weatherhead. Collegeville, Minn.: The Liturgical Press, 1975.

_____. *Springtime of the Liturgy: Liturgical Texts of the First Four Centuries*. Trans. Matthew J. O'Connell. Collegeville, Minn.: The Liturgical Press, 1979.

Hamman, Adalbert, O.F.M., ed. *Baptism: Ancient Liturgies and Patristic Texts*. English editorial supervisor: Thomas Halton. Staten Island, N.Y.: Alba House, 1968.

_____. *The Mass: Ancient Liturgies and Patristic Texts*. English editorial supervisor: Thomas Halton. Staten Island, N.Y.: Alba House, 1967.

_____. *The Paschal Mystery: Ancient Liturgies and Patristic Texts*. English editorial supervisor: Thomas Halton. Staten Island, N.Y.: Alba House, 1969.

Underhill, Evelyn, ed. *Eucharistic Prayers from the Ancient Liturgies*. New York: Longmans, Green and Co., 1939.

### Dictionaries

Davies, J. G., ed. *The New Westminster Dictionary of Liturgy and Worship*. Philadelphia: Westminster Press, 1986.

Day, Peter D. *The Liturgical Dictionary of Eastern Christianity.* Collegeville, Minn.: The Liturgical Press, 1993

Fink, Peter E., ed. *The New Dictionary of Sacramental Worship.* Collegeville, Minn.: The Liturgical Press, 1990

Komonchak, Joseph A., Mary Collins, and Dermot A. Lane. *The New Dictionary of Theology.* Wilmington, Del.: Michael Glazier, 1987.

O'Brien, T. C., ed. *Corpus Dictionary of Western Churches.* Washington, D.C.: Corpus Publications, 1970.

Rahner, Karl, and Herbert Vorgrimler. *Dictionary of Theology,* 2nd ed. Trans. Richard Strachan and others. New York: Crossroad, 1985

_____, ed. *Encyclopedia of Theology: The Concise Sacramentum mundi.* New York: Seabury, 1975.

# Glossary

**Allegory:** saying one thing to signify another. In liturgical commentaries, allegory describes the celebrants and rites as representing other realities: the deacons hold the place of the angels, the paschal candle represents the pillar of fire that guided the Hebrew people in the desert (Exod 13:21). The use of allegory is one of the conventions used in biblical and liturgical commentaries.

**Anamnesis:** a recalling of the steps of salvation history in the Old Testament, the life of Christ, and the time of the Church. Liturgical prayers usually contain such evocations; the remembrance of God's past favors emboldens the petitioner to ask for new ones.

**Anaphora:** Eucharistic Prayer. The term is used chiefly with regard to Eastern liturgies.

**Antiphonal:** a book containing the text of antiphons, or refrains of psalms; in a wider sense, the text and the melody of liturgical chants.

**Catechumenate:** the preparation for baptism of a group of candidates in order to instruct them in a liturgical setting and insure the conversion of their morals.

**Church Order:** a manual containing rules for Christian life, church discipline, and liturgical forms, often attributed to the twelve apostles.

**Deaconess:** a female auxiliary of the deacon. She deals with women for the baptismal anointing, the visit of the sick, and the assistance of the needy.

**Doxology:** a formula of praise. It is usually the conclusion of liturgical prayers, for example, "Glory to God forever!"

**Epiclesis:** an invocation within a liturgical prayer to ask for the gift and presence of the Holy Spirit—for instance in behalf of a person—or its intervention for the sanctification of elements such as the eucharistic gifts of bread and wine or the baptismal water and oil.

**Euchologion:** either all the prayers offered and directions given during a liturgical celebration, or a book containing the text of these prayers and directions (but without the readings or chants).

**Formulary:** the liturgical texts of an office or a feast, apart from the readings. **Mass Formulary:** the collection of variable pieces used in the celebration of Mass for a given day (formularies for the Mass of Easter, of Epiphany, of Sts. Peter and Paul, of St. Lawrence, and so on).

**Gradual:** either the antiphon (refrain) and psalm (at least one verse) sung after a biblical reading, or a book containing these choral responses.

**Iconoclasm:** opposition to the representation of God and the saints, going as far as destroying these images. Such a movement arose in the Byzantine church in 726 and continued until 843, in spite of the Council of Nicaea II in 787.

**Liturgy:** in the Byzantine churches, the term designating the eucharistic celebration; in the Western churches, used in a wider sense since the nineteenth century to designate the whole of Christian worship.

**Myron:** the perfumed oil used in the anointing after baptism.

**Mystagogy:** a commentary or interpretation of the liturgical celebrations. The mystagogic catecheses consisted in the explanation of baptism, chrismation (the equivalent of confirmation), and the Eucharist, for the benefit of the newly baptized who had partaken for the first time of these "holy mysteries."

**Mystery:** in the Bible, a concept designating the whole of salvation worked by God, progressively revealed and realized in the course of time and brought to its perfect fulfillment by Christ (see Eph 3:2-9). In Eastern Christianity, when used in the plural, the expression "the holy mysteries" is applied to what Western

Christianity designates by the term "sacrament." The term "mysteries" is also employed to speak of the medieval plays in the West that represented biblical stories read during the liturgy.

**Neophytes:**   the newly baptized who received special teaching (the mystagogic catecheses) during paschal week.

**Office:**   in the general sense, a liturgical celebration; in the particular sense, the celebration of each of the liturgical Hours.

**Presanctified:**   bread and wine that have been consecrated and reserved for a Communion service. In the present Roman liturgy, the celebration of Good Friday does not include a Mass, but only the Communion of the Presanctified from the Holy Thursday Mass. The Byzantine churches have a Liturgy of the Presanctified on weekdays of Lent.

**Sacramentary:**   a book containing the prayers and instructions that belong to the bishop, the presbyters, the deacon, and the acolyte. And principally a collection of formularies of Masses, arranged according to the annual cycle.

**Station (Stational Mass):**   in Rome during the first millennium one of the great basilicas or a neighborhood church where the clergy and people gathered around the pope for the liturgy on major solemnities (Christmas, Epiphany, Easter, Pentecost) and during Lent and Paschal Time. The "stational church" was the one in which the liturgical assembly took place on a given day; on the way to this church, all participants formed a procession.

**Synaxis:**   the assembly formed by a Christian community, essentially for liturgical celebrations.